Jump Start Your Own Business

12 Steps to Independence

MindStorm Publications

Table Of Contents

Introduction

Earlier in my career, I thought I had it all figured out. I was ambitious, smart, energetic, and I was ready to escape the grind of the corporate world. The idea of starting my own business seemed like the perfect ticket to freedom. So, I took the leap. I invested all our savings into my first venture. And it failed. Not just a minor setback, but a full-on disaster. Bankruptcy hit hard. We lost our home, our car, and almost everything else. It was a tough pill to swallow. But that failure turned out to be the best lesson I ever learned.

This book is for anyone who dreams of breaking free from the constraints of their current job. It's for early retirees, empty-nesters, people with and idea for a new product or service, and people eager to explore alternatives to the traditional career path. My goal is to provide you with a practical, easy-to-understand guide to starting your own business. I want to motivate, support, and guide you through actionable steps, real-world examples, and insights gleaned from my five decades of entrepreneurial experience.

One of the unique features of this book is its structure. Each chapter begins with summary bullet points, giving you a quick overview of what to expect. Real-life case studies provide concrete examples of success and failure. You'll find templates and practical tools to help you along the way. This isn't just a theoretical guide; it's a hands-on manual designed to set you up for success.

So, who exactly is this book for? If you're looking to gain independence from traditional work, this book is for you. Early retirees and empty-nesters looking for new ventures will find it particularly useful. Young people eager to explore entrepreneurship will also benefit. If you're tired of feeling stuck and want to chart your own course, you're in the right place.

Let's take a quick look at the 12 steps we'll cover:

1) **Finding Your Idea:** How to identify a business idea that excites you and meets market needs. Think about you enjoy doing, not what makes more money. If you don't enjoy it, you won't stick to it long enough to become profitable.

2) **Market Research:** Techniques for understanding your target market and competition.

3) **Business Planning:** Crafting a solid business plan that outlines your goals and strategies. Be sure to plan for a balance of work, family and health though. Without that balance, you will burn out fail to reach your intended goal.

4) **Funding Your Venture:** Exploring different funding options from bootstrapping to investors.

5) **Legalities and Licenses:** Navigating the legal requirements and obtaining necessary licenses.

6) **Building a Brand:** Creating a strong brand identity that resonates with your audience.

7) **Setting Up Operations:** Organizing the day-to-day operations to keep your business running smoothly.

8) **Marketing Strategies:** Effective marketing techniques to attract and retain customers.

9) **Sales Techniques:** Proven sales strategies to boost your revenue.

10) **Customer Service:** Building strong relationships with your customers through exceptional service.

11) **Scaling Up:** Strategies for growing your business and expanding your reach.

12) **Sustaining Success:** Tips for maintaining your business and adapting to future challenges.

A brief insight into my journey: my academic path began with a BS in Electrical Engineering & Computer Science from the University of California at Berkeley in 1972, a memorable year that also saw me getting married on the day of my graduation — a partnership that has endured for over half a century. The initial setback of my first business venture, leading to bankruptcy, steered me towards pursuing an MBA from Pepperdine, laying down the cornerstone of my business acumen. This educational foundation was pivotal as I ventured into creating a dozen businesses over five decades, experiencing a spectrum from modest successes to ventures that significantly contributed to my financial freedom, allowing for a comfortable retirement in Hawaii, and the ability to travel to 103 countries so far, including eight years of living in Ecuador as an expat to absorb the culture there.

This rollercoaster ride of entrepreneurial endeavors has been a rich source of insights and lessons, all of which I'm eager to pass on to you through this book. Starting a business is not easy. There will be challenges and setbacks. But with the right guidance and determination, you can achieve your entrepreneurial goals. I'm here to reassure you that it's possible. This book is designed to support you every step of the way. So take that first step. Dive into the chapters ahead, and start building the business of your dreams.

You've got this. Let's get started.

Chapter 1

Laying the Foundation

When I first tried to break free from the corporate world, I was full of dreams and thought I had the perfect plan. Instead, when I first attempted to carve my own path outside of the corporate realm, I encountered overwhelming challenges that led to bankruptcy, resulted in the loss of my home, and even saw me without a car. I remember sitting on the floor of our tiny home, wondering how everything had gone so wrong. Yet, that moment was the start of something greater than I could have imagined. That failure, as devastating as it was, taught me lessons beyond what any business school ever could. This chapter is about setting the right foundation for your entrepreneurial journey, and it starts with addressing one of the biggest hurdles you'll face: the fear of failure.

In this chapter, we explore:

- Conquering the Fear of Failure
- Establishing Clear Business Objectives
- Discovering and Confirming Your Business Concept
- Cultivating a Robust Mindset for Entrepreneurship

1.1 Overcoming the Fear of Failure

Fear of failure is something every entrepreneur deals with. It's like an unwelcome guest that shows up just when you're about to take the plunge. But here's the thing: fear is normal. It doesn't mean you're inadequate or that your ideas aren't good enough. In fact, it's quite the opposite. Fear shows that you're stepping out of your comfort zone, daring to do something different. Did you know that about 1 in 4 U.S. businesses fail within their first year? (Source: LendingTree) It's a daunting statistic, but it's also a reminder that failure is a common part of the entrepreneurial landscape.

Even the most successful entrepreneurs have faced their share of failures. Bill Gates' first company, Traf-O-Data, was a flop, but it laid the groundwork for Microsoft. Steve Jobs was famously fired from Apple, only to return and transform it into one of the most valuable companies in the world. Arianna Huffington faced nearly 40 rejections for her second book before founding The Huffington Post. These examples show that failure isn't the end; it's just a step in the journey.

So, how do you manage and mitigate this fear? Start with mindfulness. When fear creeps in, take a few minutes to breathe deeply and center yourself. Journaling is another powerful tool. Write down your fears and examine them. Sometimes, seeing your worries on paper can make them seem less overwhelming. Professional therapy can also offer valuable insights and coping mechanisms. Tim Ferriss, a well-known entrepreneur, practices an exercise called "fear-setting" (Source: Tim Ferriss) It involves defining your worst-case scenario, identifying steps to recover if it happens, and weighing the benefits of taking the risk. This method can help you confront your fears head-on and make more informed decisions.

Embracing failure can actually be a stepping stone to success. Take Thomas Edison, who failed over a thousand times before inventing the light bulb. Each failure taught him something new, bringing him closer to his goal. What can you learn from these setbacks? Maybe your business plan needs tweaking, or perhaps your target market isn't as interested as you thought. These lessons are invaluable and can guide you toward a more successful venture.

A growth mindset is crucial in this process. Instead of seeing challenges as insurmountable obstacles, view them as opportunities for growth. Carol Dweck, a renowned psychologist, emphasizes the power of a growth mindset in achieving success. By focusing on what you can learn from each experience, you build resilience. Try daily exercises to foster this mindset. Reflect on a challenge you faced and write down what you learned from it. Over time, this practice can shift your perspective and help you approach problems with a solution-oriented mindset.

Remember, every entrepreneur faces fear and failure. What sets successful ones apart is their ability to learn from these experiences and keep moving forward. This chapter is about laying a strong foundation for your business by addressing these fears head-on and embracing the lessons that come with failure. By doing so, you'll be better equipped to navigate the challenges ahead and turn your dreams into reality.

1.2 Setting Clear Business Goals

When I first started out, I didn't realize the importance of setting clear goals. I had big dreams but no concrete plan. It was like trying to navigate a ship without a map. Over time, I learned that setting SMART goals—Specific, Measurable, Achievable, Relevant, and Time-bound—was crucial. SMART goals give you a clear direction, helping you move from vague aspirations to tangible outcomes. For example, instead of saying, "I want to grow my business," a SMART goal would be, "I want to increase my monthly revenue by 20% over the next six months by focusing on online sales."

Let's break down each component of SMART goals. Specific goals are clear and detailed, leaving no room for ambiguity. They answer the questions of who, what, where, when, and why. Measurable goals include metrics to track your progress. Achievable goals are realistic, taking into account your resources and constraints. Relevant goals align with your broader business objectives. Time-bound goals have deadlines, creating a sense of urgency and focus. For instance, a poorly defined goal might be, "I want more customers." A SMART goal would be, "I aim to acquire 50 new customers within three months by launching a targeted social media campaign."

Setting short-term and long-term goals is essential for keeping your business on track. Short-term goals focus on immediate tasks and milestones, while long-term goals look at your broader vision. For example, a six-month goal might be to launch your website and attract your first 100 customers. A one-year goal could be to break even financially. A five-year goal might involve expanding to multiple locations or diversifying your product line. Using templates can help you outline these goals clearly. Write down your 6-month, 1-year, and 5-year goals, and revisit them regularly to track your progress.

Tracking and adjusting your goals is just as important as setting them. Life is unpredictable, and your business will face unexpected challenges and opportunities. Tools like Trello or Asana can help you keep track of your goals and tasks. These apps allow you to create boards for different projects, set deadlines, and monitor your progress. Regular review sessions—monthly or quarterly—can help you assess where you stand and make necessary adjustments. For example, if you find that you're not meeting your sales targets, you can analyze what's going wrong and tweak your strategies accordingly.

Aligning your personal and business goals can significantly enhance your motivation and satisfaction. When your business goals reflect your personal values and aspirations, you're more likely to stay committed. For instance, if one of your personal goals is to have more family time, you might set a business goal to automate certain processes, freeing up your schedule. Exercises like journaling about your values and how they intersect with your business can be incredibly insightful. Reflect on what matters most to you and how your business can support those priorities.

Consider the story of Sarah, a single mother who wanted to start a business to gain financial independence and spend more time with her kids. She set clear, aligned goals: launch an online store within six months, achieve $5,000 in monthly sales within a year, and eventually hire a small team to handle operations. By aligning her business goals with her personal desire for more family time, she stayed motivated and focused. She used goal-tracking apps to monitor her progress and adjusted her strategies as needed, achieving her targets and creating a balanced life.

Setting clear business goals is not just about ticking boxes; it's about creating a roadmap that guides you towards your vision while keeping you grounded in reality. By adopting the SMART framework, differentiating between short-term and long-term objectives, and regularly tracking and adjusting your goals, you set yourself up for success. Aligning your personal and business aspirations ensures that your entrepreneurial journey is fulfilling on both professional and personal fronts.

1.3 Identifying and Validating Your Business Idea

The spark of a great business often starts with an idea. But how do you know if your idea is viable? Start by brainstorming. Let your creativity flow without judgment. Techniques like mind mapping can help. Write your main idea in the center of a page and draw branches for related concepts. This visual approach can reveal connections you hadn't considered. Another useful method is SWOT analysis—identifying strengths, weaknesses, opportunities, and threats. It's a strategic way to assess the potential of your idea. Customer surveys are also invaluable. Ask people what they need, what problems they face, and how your idea could help. This feedback can refine your concept and make it more appealing.

Successful businesses often start with simple ideas. Take Airbnb, for example. It began as a way for the founders to make extra money by renting out air mattresses in their apartment. They identified a need—affordable lodging—and turned it into a multi-billion-dollar company. Similarly, Spanx started with Sara Blakely cutting the feet off her pantyhose to wear under white pants. Her simple solution to a common problem led to a revolutionary product line. These stories show that the best ideas often come from solving everyday issues.

Once you have an idea, the next step is market research. Understanding your market validates your idea and gives you insights into your competition. Start with primary research—directly gathering information from potential customers. This can be through interviews, surveys, or focus groups. Secondary research involves analyzing existing data like industry reports and market studies. Tools like Google Trends can help identify market trends, while websites like Statista provide valuable industry statistics. Competitor analysis is crucial. Identify your main competitors and study their strengths and weaknesses. What are they doing well? Where are they falling short? This analysis can help you position your business more effectively.

Testing and validating your idea before full-scale implementation is essential. Start with a Minimum Viable Product (MVP). This is the simplest version of your product that can still solve the core problem. It allows you to gather feedback and make improvements without a massive investment. For example, Dropbox started with a simple video demonstrating its concept. The positive feedback validated the idea before they built the full product. Running pilot programs or focus groups can also provide valuable insights. These small-scale tests help you understand how your target audience interacts with your product and what improvements are needed.

Identifying a unique value proposition is another critical step. Your value proposition is what sets you apart from the competition. It's the unique benefit that only your product or service provides. Start by asking yourself what problem your business solves and why your solution is better than others. Crafting a clear, concise value proposition statement can help. Use a template that includes your target audience, the problem you're solving, and the unique benefits of your solution. For example, Slack's value proposition is "Be More Productive at Work with Less Effort." It clearly states the benefit and appeals to its target audience—professionals seeking productivity.

Consider businesses with strong, distinctive value propositions. Dollar Shave Club disrupted the razor market with its simple, cost-effective subscription model, making shaving easier and cheaper for men. They identified a gap in the market and offered a unique solution. Similarly, Warby Parker provides stylish, affordable eyewear with a home try-on program, solving the hassle of buying glasses. Their value proposition is clear and resonates with their target audience. By focusing on what makes your idea unique and valuable, you can stand out in a crowded market.

Identifying and validating your business idea is a crucial step in building a successful venture. By encouraging creativity, conducting thorough market research, testing your concept, and crafting a unique value proposition, you can turn a simple idea into a thriving business. The journey may be challenging, but with the right approach and mindset, you can navigate the path to entrepreneurial success.

1.4 Building a Resilient Entrepreneurial Mindset

Resilience is the backbone of entrepreneurship. It keeps you going when the odds are stacked against you. A resilient entrepreneur embodies several key traits. First, there's adaptability. The business world is ever-changing, and being able to pivot when necessary is crucial. Think of Reed Hastings, the co-founder of Netflix. When he realized that DVD rentals were becoming obsolete, he pivoted the company towards streaming. This adaptability transformed Netflix into a global powerhouse.

Perseverance is another hallmark of resilience. It's about pushing through obstacles, no matter how daunting. Consider J.K. Rowling, who faced numerous rejections before finally publishing the Harry Potter series. Her perseverance paid off, making her one of the most successful authors in history. Optimism also plays a significant role. It's not about ignoring challenges but maintaining a positive outlook and believing in your ability to overcome them. Elon Musk, despite facing countless setbacks with SpaceX and Tesla, remains optimistic about the future. His belief in his vision keeps him moving forward.

Continuous learning and self-improvement are vital for staying relevant and thriving. The business landscape evolves rapidly, and staying informed is crucial. Read books like "The Lean Startup" by Eric Ries or "Good to Great" by Jim Collins. Listen to podcasts such as "How I Built This" by NPR, which features stories from successful entrepreneurs. Enroll in online courses on platforms like Coursera or Udemy to keep your skills sharp. Setting up a personal development plan can help. Allocate time each week for learning new skills, attending webinars, or reading industry-related articles. This commitment to growth ensures you're always prepared for whatever comes your way.

Staying motivated during tough times can be challenging. Surround yourself with a support system. Mentors can provide invaluable advice and perspective. Peer groups offer camaraderie and shared experiences. Daily routines can also boost motivation. Start your day with a morning routine that includes exercise, meditation, and reading. Break your tasks into manageable chunks and celebrate small wins. These habits can keep you energized and focused.

Self-care is crucial for maintaining resilience. Entrepreneurship can be demanding, and neglecting your well-being can lead to burnout. Regular exercise is a great way to keep your energy levels up. Whether it's a morning jog, a yoga session, or a gym workout, find something you enjoy and make it a part of your routine. Meditation and mindfulness practices can help manage stress and improve mental clarity. Apps like Headspace or Calm offer guided sessions that can fit into your schedule.

Maintaining a work-life balance is also important. Set boundaries between work and personal time. Designate specific hours for work and stick to them. Make time for hobbies and activities that bring you joy. Spend quality time with family and friends. These practices can rejuvenate you and provide the mental space needed to tackle business challenges. Stress management techniques, such as deep breathing exercises or taking regular breaks, can also help keep stress levels in check.

Building a resilient entrepreneurial mindset involves cultivating adaptability, perseverance, and optimism. It requires a commitment to continuous learning and self-improvement. Staying motivated and maintaining self-care practices are also crucial. By embracing these principles, you can navigate the ups and downs of entrepreneurship with confidence and resilience.

As you move forward, remember that each challenge is an opportunity to grow. Building a business is not just about achieving financial success; it's about personal growth and resilience. Embrace the journey, learn from every experience, and keep pushing forward. The road may be tough, but with the right mindset, you can turn your dreams into reality.

Chapter 2

Crafting Your Business Plan

We will next explore what goes into creating your personal business plan:

- Designing a Persuasive Vision and Mission Statement
- Executing Comprehensive Market Analysis
- Constructing a Feasible Financial Strategy
- Drafting a Thorough Business Plan Outline

Imagine this moment: you're sitting at your kitchen table, a cup of coffee in hand, and a notebook in front of you. The house is quiet, and your mind is buzzing with ideas. You've decided to take the leap and start your own business. But where do you start? The foundation of any successful business is a well-crafted business plan. It's your roadmap, guiding you from a simple idea to a thriving enterprise. Let's dive into the first step of creating this plan: crafting a compelling vision and mission statement.

2.1 Crafting a Compelling Vision and Mission Statement

A vision statement is like a lighthouse guiding your business through the foggy waters of uncertainty. It outlines what you aspire to become in the future, providing a sense of direction and purpose. A clear vision is not just a lofty idea; it's crucial for long-term success. It keeps you focused and motivated, especially during challenging times. Take IKEA's vision, for instance: "To create a better everyday life for the many people." This simple yet powerful statement not only guides their business decisions but also resonates with their customers worldwide.

Crafting your vision statement starts with reflecting on your personal and business aspirations. Ask yourself, "What do I want to achieve with this business? How do I see it impacting the world in the next ten or twenty years?" Take some time to write down your thoughts. Don't rush this process. Your vision should be unique and bold, something that excites you and your team. Engage your partners, managers, and employees in this brainstorming session. Their insights can add depth and perspective to your vision.

Once you've clarified your vision, the next step is to create a mission statement. While a vision statement focuses on the future, a mission statement is about the present. It defines your business's purpose, values, and goals. It's a concise declaration of why your business exists and what it stands for. Let's break it down: your mission statement should include your purpose (why you do what you do), your values (the principles that guide your actions), and your goals (what you aim to achieve). For example, TED's mission statement is "Spread ideas." It's simple, clear, and communicates their purpose effectively.

To craft an impactful mission statement, start by identifying your business's core purpose. What problem are you solving? Why does it matter? Next, define your values. These are the principles that will guide your decisions and actions. Finally, outline your goals. These should be specific and actionable, giving your team a clear direction. Consider the mission statement of Warby Parker: "We believe that buying glasses should be easy and fun. It should leave you happy and good-looking, with money in your pocket. We also believe that everyone has the right to see." It's a powerful blend of purpose, values, and goals.

It's important to understand the difference between a vision and a mission statement. While they are closely related, they serve distinct purposes. A vision statement is aspirational, focusing on what you want to become in the future. It's broad and long-term. On the other hand, a mission statement is operational, detailing your current purpose and activities. It's specific and actionable. Think of your vision statement as the destination and your mission statement as the path to get there.

Here's a quick comparison to help you differentiate:

- **Vision Statement:** Future-focused, aspirational, provides long-term direction.
- **Mission Statement:** Present-focused, operational, outline's purpose and goals.

To help you create your own vision and mission statements, I've included some fill-in-the-blank templates. For your vision statement, try: "To become [aspirational goal] for [target audience] by [unique approach]." For example, "To become the leading provider of eco-friendly products for environmentally conscious consumers by innovating sustainable solutions." For your mission statement, use: "Our mission is to [core purpose] by [specific actions] while [values]." For example, "Our mission is to provide high-quality, affordable education to underprivileged children by partnering with local communities while promoting inclusivity and diversity."

Here are some examples to inspire you. Consider Google's vision: "To provide access to the world's information in one click." It's ambitious yet clear. Or take a look at Whole Foods' mission: "To nourish people and the planet." It succinctly captures their purpose and values.

Crafting a compelling vision and mission statement is a crucial step in building a strong foundation for your business. These statements provide clarity, motivation, and direction, guiding your decisions and actions. They align your team around a shared purpose and inspire your customers. So take your time, reflect deeply, and create statements that truly resonate with your aspirations and values. This is your opportunity to articulate your dreams and set the stage for your business's success.

2.2 Conducting Effective Market Research

Understanding your market is like having a map in unfamiliar territory. Without it, you're navigating blind. Market research provides you with invaluable insights that inform your strategic decisions, helping you avoid costly mistakes. Consider the story of Netflix. Before they shifted their focus from DVD rentals to streaming, they conducted extensive market research. They discovered that consumers were increasingly interested in on-demand entertainment. This insight was pivotal, allowing Netflix to pivot successfully and dominate the streaming industry. Thorough market research can mean the difference between sinking and swimming in the business world.

Primary market research involves gathering firsthand information directly from potential customers. This hands-on approach gives you fresh, targeted data tailored to your specific needs. One effective method is surveys. Create a list of questions that glean insights into customer preferences, needs, and pain points. For instance, if you're launching a new fitness app, you might ask, "What features do you find most useful in a fitness app?" or "How much are you willing to pay for a premium subscription?" Tools like Google Forms or SurveyMonkey can help you distribute these surveys easily. Another method is conducting interviews. Sit down with potential customers and have a conversation. This can be more revealing as it allows for follow-up questions and deeper insights. Focus groups are also valuable. Gather a small group of target customers and discuss your product or service. Observe their reactions and take note of their feedback. These techniques provide a wealth of qualitative data that can shape your business strategy.

Secondary market research involves analyzing existing data to gain market insights. This data is often readily available and can provide a broader view of the market landscape. Start by looking at industry reports and market studies. Websites like Statista and IBISWorld offer comprehensive reports on various industries. These reports can help you understand market trends, competitive landscapes, and consumer behaviors. Another valuable source is government and trade publications. These often contain valuable statistics and insights. For example, the U.S. Small Business Administration (SBA) provides a wealth of data on small business trends. Tools like Google Trends can also be helpful. They allow you to see how often specific search terms are used, providing insights into consumer interests and market trends.

Analyzing and interpreting research findings is where the magic happens. It's about making sense of the data to inform your business strategies. Start by identifying patterns and trends. Look for recurring themes in your survey responses or interview notes. For example, if multiple respondents mention a need for a particular feature in your app, that's a clear indicator of demand. Use tools like Excel or Google Sheets to organize and analyze your data. Create charts and graphs to visualize the information. This can make it easier to spot patterns and draw insights.

Once you've identified key insights, the next step is to use them to shape your business decisions. For example, if your research reveals a strong demand for eco-friendly products, you might decide to source sustainable materials or highlight your green practices in your marketing. Or, if you discover that your target market prefers online shopping, you might focus on enhancing your e-commerce platform. Real-world examples abound. Consider Coca-Cola. They used market research to understand consumer preferences and introduced Diet Coke, which became a massive success. Similarly, LEGO conducted extensive research to understand why their sales were declining. They discovered that kids were spending more time on digital devices. In response, they launched LEGO video games and online platforms, revitalizing their brand.

Conducting market research might seem daunting, but it's a crucial step in building a successful business. It provides the insights needed to make informed decisions, avoid pitfalls, and seize opportunities. By gathering firsthand information through surveys, interviews, and focus groups, and analyzing existing data from industry reports and market studies, you can create a solid foundation for your business. Use these insights to guide your strategies, ensuring they're aligned with market needs and trends. This way, you're not just guessing—you're making data-driven decisions that increase your chances of success.

2.3 Developing a Realistic Financial Plan

Creating a solid financial plan is like building the backbone of your business. It ensures you're not just dreaming but setting realistic, achievable goals. The components of a financial plan include revenue projections, expense forecasts, and profit margins. Revenue projections estimate how much money you expect to bring in. They're based on market research, your pricing strategy, and sales forecasts. Expense forecasts, on the other hand, detail all your expected costs, from office rent to marketing expenses. Profit margins are the difference between your revenue and expenses, showing how much profit you're likely to make. Visual aids like charts and graphs can make these projections clearer. They help you visualize your financial trajectory, making it easier to spot trends and make informed decisions.

Creating a startup budget is the next crucial step. Start by listing all your initial expenses. These might include equipment, technology, office space, and marketing. For instance, if you're starting a café, your costs could range from coffee machines and furniture to initial stock and marketing campaigns. Use a template to organize these expenses. Divide them into categories like fixed costs (rent, salaries) and variable costs (inventory, utilities). This helps you see where your money is going and identify areas where you can cut costs. Common startup expenses vary by industry. A tech startup might spend more on software and development tools, while a retail business might invest heavily in inventory and store setup.

Managing cash flow is vital for keeping your business afloat. Cash flow is the money moving in and out of your business. Positive cash flow means you have more money coming in than going out, which is crucial for covering expenses and investing in growth. One effective strategy is to invoice promptly and follow up on late payments. Tools like QuickBooks or FreshBooks can automate invoicing and help you track payments. Expense tracking is another key aspect. Regularly review your expenses and look for ways to save. For example, negotiate better terms with suppliers or switch to more cost-effective service providers. Tools like Expensify can simplify expense tracking, making it easier to stay on top of your finances.

When it comes to funding your business, you have several options. Equity financing involves selling a portion of your business in exchange for capital. This could be through angel investors or venture capitalists. It's a great way to raise significant funds, but it means giving up some control. Loans are another option. They allow you to retain full ownership but come with the obligation of repayment with interest. Grants are non-repayable funds, often provided by government agencies or non-profits. They're competitive but can be a valuable source of funding without the burden of debt. Preparing a funding pitch is crucial when approaching investors. Your pitch should clearly outline your business, the problem it solves, your target market, and your financial projections. Practice your pitch until you can deliver it confidently and succinctly. Tailor it to your audience, addressing their potential concerns and highlighting the benefits.

In the early days of one of my ventures, I remember the anxiety of waiting for a loan approval. It felt like everything hinged on that decision. But having a well-prepared pitch and clear financial plan made all the difference. The bank saw the potential and approved the loan, giving us the boost we needed. However, we didn't stop there. We kept a close eye on our cash flow, using tools to track every dollar. This vigilance paid off, allowing us to catch issues early and make adjustments before they became problems.

Developing a realistic financial plan involves understanding your revenue, forecasting your expenses, and managing your cash flow effectively. By creating a detailed startup budget, you can identify and control your costs. Exploring various funding options and preparing a solid pitch can secure the capital you need to launch and grow. This financial foundation not only supports your business but also gives you the confidence to navigate the complexities of entrepreneurship.

2.4 Creating a Detailed Business Plan Template

When I first started out, I didn't realize how crucial a detailed business plan was. It's more than just a document; it's your roadmap, your guide through the often-turbulent waters of entrepreneurship. A comprehensive business plan provides structure and clarity, not just for you, but for potential investors and partners too. Let's break down the sections you'll need to include, ensuring your plan is robust and convincing.

Start with the executive summary. This is the first thing people will read, so it needs to be engaging and concise. Think of it as your elevator pitch on paper. Capture the essence of your business: what you do, who you serve, and how you stand out. Include your mission statement, brief product or service description, and key financial projections. For instance, "Our mission is to revolutionize home fitness with affordable, high-quality equipment. We aim to achieve $1 million in revenue within the first year by targeting health-conscious consumers." This sets the stage and piques interest.

Next, dive into your business model. Describe how your business operates and makes money. Are you a subscription-based service, a retail store, or perhaps an online marketplace? Detail your revenue streams, pricing strategy, and distribution channels. Imagine you're launching an online clothing store. Explain your sourcing process, the technology behind your e-commerce platform, and your customer service approach. The clearer you are, the better your plan can guide you and convince others of its viability.

Market analysis is your chance to show you've done your homework. Present data on your industry, target market, and competitors. Use graphs and charts to illustrate market trends and consumer behavior. If you're opening a café in a busy neighborhood, include demographic data, local coffee shop competition, and consumer preferences. Highlight any gaps in the market that your business will fill. This section proves you understand the landscape and have a strategy to thrive within it.

Financial projections are the backbone of your business plan. Include revenue forecasts, expense budgets, and profit margins. Use visual aids like bar graphs and pie charts to make these numbers digestible. For example, project your sales for the first five years, breaking down your expected revenue growth. Detail your startup costs, such as equipment, initial stock, and marketing expenses, to show you've planned meticulously. Investors need to see that your business is financially viable and that you've thought through every penny.

Writing each section of your business plan requires attention to detail. For the executive summary, be compelling but succinct. Capture the reader's attention and provide a snapshot of your business. When describing your products or services, focus on the benefits. What problem do they solve? Why should customers choose you over competitors? Use clear, straightforward language that anyone can understand. For instance, instead of saying, "Our product leverages advanced algorithms to optimize user experience," say, "Our product uses smart technology to make your life easier."

Offering examples of well-written business plans can be incredibly helpful. Let's consider a tech startup and a retail store. The tech startup's executive summary might highlight its innovative software and market potential, while the retail store's might focus on location and unique product offerings. Annotated examples can illustrate key elements like a strong value proposition, a clear market analysis, and realistic financial projections. Comparing traditional business plans with lean startup plans can also be instructive. Traditional plans are detailed and comprehensive, ideal for securing funding. Lean startup plans are concise and flexible, perfect for quickly testing and iterating business ideas.

A business plan is not static; it's a living document that should evolve with your business. Regularly review and update it to reflect new insights, market changes, or shifts in your strategy. Schedule quarterly reviews to assess your progress and make necessary adjustments. Use tools like business plan software to track changes and maintain a clear, organized document. This ongoing revision process ensures your plan stays relevant and continues to guide your decisions effectively.

Creating a detailed business plan is a critical step in launching and running a successful business. It provides structure, clarity, and a clear path forward. By outlining each section with care, using real-world examples, and keeping the plan updated, you set yourself up for success. A well-crafted business plan is your blueprint, guiding you from concept to reality and beyond.

Chapter 3

Legal and Administrative Essentials

Every business must understand and follow these essential elements:

- Crafting a Compelling Vision and Mission Statement
- Conducting an In-depth Market Analysis
- Developing a Realistic Financial Strategy
- Creating a Detailed Business Plan Framework

When I first started my own business, I was overwhelmed by the legal and administrative tasks. It felt like navigating a maze with no map. Understanding the legal framework is crucial for any new business owner, whether you're an early retiree looking for a new challenge, an empty-nester ready to venture into entrepreneurship, or a young person eager to break free from the corporate grind. as I was. Let's dive into the different types of business structures and how to choose the right one for you.

3.1 Choosing the Right Business Structure

The first step in setting up your business is deciding on its structure. The structure you choose will impact your daily operations, taxes, liability, and even your ability to raise money. There are several options, each with its own set of characteristics.

A Sole Proprietorship represents the most straightforward and commonly adopted structure for small businesses. Its simplicity facilitates easy formation and grants you unparalleled control over your business operations. However, this structure does not establish your business as a separate legal entity, leaving your personal assets vulnerable in the event of business debts or legal challenges. While perfect for those embarking on small-scale ventures and preferring a direct approach, its appeal to investors is limited due to the lack of a formal business entity. Reflecting on my personal experience, opting for a sole proprietorship in my initial business venture led to significant financial repercussions, including personal bankruptcy and the loss of nearly all personal assets, following the business's failure.

A Partnership represents a straightforward path for businesses with multiple owners. This structure is divided into two primary categories: Limited Partnerships (LP) and Limited Liability Partnerships (LLP). In an LP, one partner bears unlimited liability, while the others enjoy limited liability but also limited control over the business. Conversely, an LLP affords all partners limited liability, safeguarding personal assets against the business's debts. Partnerships excel in fostering a collaborative environment with pooled resources, yet they carry the inherent risk of internal conflicts. Moreover, the question of liability remains a crucial consideration for all involved. Drawing from broader business observations, it's evident that even the strongest partnerships can face challenges, as financial stakes and control issues can strain the most robust relationships. For this reason, I have personally avoided this form of business organization.

A Limited Liability Company (LLC) combines the benefits of a corporation and a partnership. It protects your personal assets in most cases, and profits and losses pass through to your personal income without corporate taxes. However, members must pay self-employment taxes for Medicare and Social Security. An LLC offers flexibility and protection, making it a popular choice for many new businesses. It requires more paperwork than a sole proprietorship but provides more security, and the taxes may be larger, depending on your personal financial situation.

Corporations are more complex and expensive to set up but offer the strongest protection against personal liability. There are different types of corporations, including C Corporations and S Corporations. A C Corporation (C Corp) is a separate legal entity, providing the most robust personal liability protection. However, profits are taxed twice— once at the corporate level and again as shareholder dividends. An S Corporation (S Corp) avoids double taxation, with profits and losses passing through to personal income. However, it must meet IRS eligibility requirements, such as having no more than 100 shareholders. Corporations are ideal for businesses planning to scale significantly and attract investors. Personally, all my serious businesses were set up as S Corps. That provided the most protection with the least amount of paperwork, and my personal financial situation did not warrant the C Corp structure.

Choosing the right structure depends on several factors. Consider the size and scope of your business. If you're starting small with minimal risk, a sole proprietorship or partnership might be sufficient. However, if you plan to grow and attract investors, an LLC or corporation might be better. Future growth plans also play a role. Think about where you see your business in five or ten years. Industry-specific requirements may dictate your choice. Some industries have regulations that favor certain structures. Finally, assess your personal risk tolerance. If protecting your personal assets is a priority, an LLC or corporation is advisable.

Once you've chosen your structure, the next step is to establish it legally. Start by filing the necessary documents with your state authorities. This often involves registering your business name and filing articles of incorporation for corporations or articles of organization for LLCs. Draft partnership agreements or operating agreements, especially for partnerships and LLCs. These documents outline the roles and responsibilities of each partner or member, helping to prevent disputes down the line.

Obtaining an Employer Identification Number (EIN) from the IRS is essential. This number is used for tax purposes and is required for hiring employees. You can apply for an EIN online through the IRS website. Finally, register for state and local taxes. Depending on your location and business type, you may need to register for sales tax, income tax, and other specific taxes. Check with your state's Department of Revenue for detailed requirements. This is actually quite simple these days, and can be completed online. Even if you are the only employee of your company, be sure to complete this step.

Choosing the right business structure is a critical decision that affects every aspect of your business. By understanding the pros and cons of each structure and considering your specific needs and goals, you can make an informed choice that sets your business up for success. The process may seem daunting, but taking it step by step ensures you cover all bases and build a solid legal foundation for your entrepreneurial venture.

3.2 Understanding Licensing and Permits

When I first decided to start my own business, I quickly realized that understanding and obtaining the correct licenses and permits was not just a formality. It's a crucial step that can make or break your business. Compliance with licensing requirements is vital for several reasons. First, it helps you avoid legal penalties that can be costly and damaging. Imagine investing your time and money into a business only to face fines or even closure for not having the right permits. Second, having the proper licenses ensures your business operates legitimately, which builds trust with customers and partners. No one wants to do business with a company that seems shady or unprofessional. Lastly, being compliant demonstrates that you're serious and committed, which can open doors to partnerships and opportunities that might otherwise be closed.

Different industries have different licensing requirements, and it's essential to know what applies to yours. For instance, if you're starting a food business, you'll need health permits to ensure you meet safety and hygiene standards. These permits are typically issued by your local health department and require regular inspections. For professional service providers like accountants, lawyers, or real estate agents, obtaining a professional license is mandatory. These licenses verify your qualifications and competency, often requiring exams and continuing education. If your business involves manufacturing, you might need environmental permits. These permits regulate emissions, waste disposal, and other environmental impacts, ensuring your operations comply with local, state, and federal environmental laws.

Researching and identifying the necessary licenses and permits can seem overwhelming, but there are practical steps you can take. Start by visiting government websites like the U.S. Small Business Administration (SBA) or your state's business portal. These sites often provide comprehensive guides and resources tailored to specific industries. Consulting with local business associations can also be helpful. These organizations are familiar with local regulations and can provide valuable insights and support. Don't hesitate to reach out to other business owners in your industry for advice. They've navigated these waters before and can offer practical tips.

Once you've identified the required licenses and permits, the next step is to apply for them. This process usually starts with completing application forms. These forms ask for detailed information about your business, including its structure, location, and nature of operations. Be thorough and accurate in your responses to avoid delays. Along with the application, you'll need to submit the required documentation. This might include proof of identity, business plans, and financial statements. The specific documents vary by license, so carefully review the application requirements.

After submitting your application, keep track of renewal dates and compliance requirements. Many licenses and permits need to be renewed periodically, and failing to do so can result in penalties or even the loss of your license. Set reminders for renewal dates and regularly check for any changes in regulations that might affect your business. Maintaining compliance is an ongoing process, not a one-time task. Regularly review your permits and licenses to ensure they're up to date and meet all regulatory requirements.

To make this process easier, consider creating a checklist of all the licenses and permits your business needs, along with their application and renewal dates. Also, enter those critical dates into your online calendar to remind you when the needed renewal dates are coming due. This simple tool can help you stay organized and ensure you don't miss any critical deadlines. For instance, if you're running a café, your checklist might include a health permit, a food handler's license, a business license, and a sales tax permit. Each item would have a column for the application date, approval date, renewal date, and any specific compliance notes.

Understanding licensing and permits is a critical step in setting up your business. It ensures compliance, builds trust, and protects you from legal issues. While the process may seem daunting, breaking it down into manageable steps—researching, applying, and maintaining—can make it much more straightforward. Remember, this is not just about ticking boxes; it's about laying a strong legal foundation for your business's long-term success. Following these steps will help you navigate the complexities of licensing and permits, allowing you to focus on growing your business with confidence.

3.3 Navigating Tax Obligations

Understanding and managing your tax obligations is a crucial part of running a business. Taxes can seem intimidating, but with the right knowledge and tools, you can handle them effectively. Let's start with an overview of the different types of taxes you'll encounter.

Income tax is a fundamental obligation. All businesses, except partnerships, must file an annual income tax return. Partnerships file an information return. The form you use depends on your business structure. For instance, sole proprietors use Schedule C, while corporations use Form 1120. Income tax is a pay-as-you-go tax, meaning you pay as you earn or receive income. This ensures you're keeping up with your tax obligations throughout the year, not just at tax time.

Sales tax is another critical tax for businesses selling products or services. If you sell taxable goods or services, you must collect sales tax from customers and remit it to the state. Each state has its own rules regarding sales tax, so it's essential to familiarize yourself with your state's requirements. Some states also have local sales taxes, adding another layer of complexity. Tools like Avalara or TaxJar can help automate sales tax collection and reporting, reducing the burden on you.

Payroll tax applies if you have employees. This includes federal and state income tax withholding, Social Security and Medicare taxes, and federal unemployment tax (FUTA). As an employer, you're responsible for withholding these taxes from your employees' wages and paying both the employee and employer portions. Keeping accurate payroll records is crucial to ensure you're compliant and to avoid costly penalties.

Self-employment tax is a must for those who are self-employed. This tax covers Social Security and Medicare contributions. Unlike employees who have these taxes withheld from their paychecks, self-employed individuals must pay both the employer and employee portions. If your net earnings from self-employment are $400 or more, you must file Schedule SE with your income tax return. This ensures you're contributing to your Social Security and Medicare benefits, which are vital for your future. For those embarking on self-employment, there's a notable advantage when it comes to Individual Retirement Accounts (IRAs). Unlike employees of companies who are capped at contributing $7,000 annually to their IRAs, self-employed individuals have the potential to contribute up to $69,000 as of 2024. This substantial difference not only offers immediate tax benefits but also significantly enhances future investment growth. Maximizing IRA contributions was a strategy I personally employed, leading to our current comfortable retirement in Hawaii.

Effective tax management requires careful planning and compliance. Start by keeping accurate financial records. This means tracking all your income and expenses meticulously. Use accounting software like QuickBooks or FreshBooks to simplify this process. These tools help you stay organized and make it easier to generate financial reports. Understanding tax deductions and credits is also crucial. Deductions reduce your taxable income, while credits reduce your tax liability. Common deductions include business expenses like office supplies, travel, and advertising. Credits might include those for energy-efficient improvements or hiring certain types of employees.

Registering with tax authorities is a crucial step in ensuring compliance. Start by applying for an Employer Identification Number (EIN) from the IRS. This number is used for tax purposes and is required if you plan to hire employees or open a business bank account. You can apply for an EIN online, and it only takes a few minutes. Next, register for state and local taxes. This often involves registering with your state's Department of Revenue and obtaining any necessary permits or licenses. Don't forget to file quarterly estimated tax payments. These payments cover your income and self-employment taxes and help you avoid penalties for underpayment.

Working with a tax professional can provide significant benefits. A qualified accountant or tax advisor can help you navigate the complexities of tax law, identify deductions and credits you might have missed, and ensure you're compliant with all regulations. When selecting a tax advisor, look for someone with experience in your industry and strong client reviews. Ask potential advisors about their credentials, experience, and approach to tax planning. Regular tax reviews with your advisor are essential. These reviews help you stay on top of your tax obligations, plan for future tax liabilities, and make informed financial decisions.

Navigating tax obligations is an integral part of running a successful business. By understanding the various types of taxes, keeping accurate records, utilizing accounting software, and working with a qualified tax professional, you can manage your tax responsibilities effectively and focus on growing your business.

3.4 Protecting Your Intellectual Property

When I first started my own business, I underestimated the importance of intellectual property (IP). It wasn't until I faced a situation where someone copied my branding that I realized how crucial it is to protect your ideas and creations. Intellectual property includes intangible assets like names, designs, and processes that are vital to your business's identity and competitive edge. There are four main types of IP: trademarks, patents, copyrights, and trade secrets, each serving a unique purpose in safeguarding your business.

Trademarks protect symbols, names, and slogans used to identify goods or services. Imagine having a unique logo or brand name that sets your business apart. A trademark ensures that no one else can use your distinctive brand elements, which helps maintain your brand's integrity and recognition. Patents protect new inventions, granting you exclusive rights to your innovation. This means no one can make, use, or sell your invention without your permission. There are different types of patents, including utility patents for new processes or machines and design patents for ornamental designs. Copyrights protect creative works like books, music, and software. If you've written a book or developed software, a copyright ensures you control how your work is used and distributed.

Trade secrets protect confidential business information that gives you a competitive advantage, like formulas or processes. Think of the Coca-Cola recipe or Google's search algorithm—these are trade secrets that are fiercely protected.

Identifying and protecting your IP is a critical step in securing your business's future. Start with a trademark search to ensure your brand elements are unique and not already in use. The United States Patent and Trademark Office (USPTO) website is a great resource for conducting this search. Once you've confirmed your brand's uniqueness, file a trademark application with the USPTO. This process involves submitting a detailed description of your trademark and paying an application fee. For patents, the process is more complex. You'll need to prepare a detailed patent application, including drawings and descriptions of your invention. It's often helpful to hire a patent attorney to navigate this process. The USPTO website offers resources and guidelines for submitting a patent application.

Registering copyrights is relatively straightforward. You can do this through the U.S. Copyright Office website. Simply fill out the appropriate forms and submit a copy of the work you want to protect. For trade secrets, the focus is on maintaining confidentiality. Implement confidentiality agreements with employees and partners, and use non-disclosure agreements (NDAs) when discussing sensitive information. These legal documents ensure that anyone with access to your trade secrets is legally bound to keep them confidential.

The legal process of IP registration varies for each type. Filing trademark applications with the USPTO involves providing a detailed description of your trademark, specifying the goods or services it will be used for, and paying the required fees. Once submitted, your application will be reviewed, and if approved, your trademark will be published in the USPTO's Official Gazette. For patents, you need to prepare and submit a detailed application to the USPTO. This includes a thorough description of your invention, accompanying drawings, and claims that define the scope of your patent. The review process can be lengthy, often taking several years. Registering copyrights with the U.S. Copyright Office is more straightforward. Fill out the necessary forms, submit a copy of your work, and pay the registration fee. Once processed, you'll receive a certificate of registration, giving you legal protection for your creative work.

Managing and enforcing your IP rights is an ongoing process. Regularly monitor for IP infringement to ensure no one is using your intellectual property without permission. This can involve setting up alerts or periodically checking relevant marketplaces and online platforms. If you discover infringement, take legal action to protect your rights. This might involve sending a cease-and-desist letter or pursuing legal proceedings. Licensing agreements are another way to manage your IP. These agreements allow others to use your IP under specific conditions, providing you with additional revenue streams. Finally, remember to renew your IP registrations. Trademarks, patents, and copyrights all have expiration dates, and renewing them ensures continued protection.

Protecting your intellectual property is a crucial aspect of running a successful business. By understanding the different types of IP, taking steps to safeguard your assets, and actively managing your rights, you can protect your business's unique identity and competitive advantage.

Navigating the legal and administrative aspects of starting a business might seem overwhelming, but taking the time to establish a solid foundation is crucial. From choosing the right business structure to protecting your intellectual property, these steps ensure your business is legally sound and set up for success.

Chapter 4
Funding Your Business

No venture can flourish without a solid foundation of funding. In this section, we delve into the critical components every entrepreneur must master:

- Defining a clear and inspiring Vision and Mission Statement
- Undertaking Comprehensive Market Research
- Formulating a Sound Financial Plan
- Constructing an In-depth Business Plan

When I was just starting out, finding the money to get my business off the ground felt like trying to catch lightning in a bottle. I didn't have investors lining up or a hefty bank account to dip into. But I did have determination and a knack for stretching every dollar. If you're looking to break free from your current job constraints, whether you're an early retiree, an empty-nester, or someone itching to start a second career, bootstrapping can be your ticket to independence.

4.1 Bootstrapping Your Startup

Bootstrapping is the art of starting and growing your business with minimal external funding. It means relying on your own savings and the revenue your business generates to keep it afloat. This approach allows you to retain full ownership and control, which means you can make decisions without answering to investors or partners. Think of it as building your empire brick by brick with your own hands. Companies like Mailchimp and Basecamp started this way. Mailchimp, founded by Ben Chestnut and Dan Kurzius, began as a side project while they ran a web design business. They reinvested their profits back into the business, targeting small businesses and using a freemium model to attract users. Today, Mailchimp is valued at over $12 billion. Similarly, Basecamp, originally a web design company called 37signals, developed its project management tool as an internal project. By focusing on profitability over growth and adopting a customer-centric approach, Basecamp now serves millions of users.

Minimizing startup costs is a cornerstone of successful bootstrapping. One practical tip is to rent equipment instead of buying it. For example, if you're starting a photography business, renting high-end cameras and lenses can save you a significant amount of money upfront. Once your business generates steady income, you can consider purchasing your own gear. Another way to cut costs is by utilizing free or low-cost software tools. Platforms like Canva for graphic design, Trello for project management, and Wave for accounting offer robust features without breaking the bank. Negotiating with suppliers for better terms can also make a big difference. When I was launching one of my ventures, I managed to negotiate a discount with a supplier by committing to a longer-term contract. These small savings added up and provided the financial cushion we needed. Even now, comfortably retired, I still leverage these free software tools to manage the finances of my book's expenses and revenue.

Generating initial capital internally is another key aspect of bootstrapping. One way to do this is by setting aside a portion of your income for business use. This might mean cutting back on non-essential expenses in your personal life to save more. When I first started, I downsized my living arrangements and cut out unnecessary subscriptions. It wasn't easy, but it freed up funds to invest in my business. Reinvesting initial profits back into the business is also crucial. Instead of pocketing your first earnings, use them to buy more inventory, improve your website, or expand your marketing efforts. This reinvestment can accelerate your growth and help you reach profitability faster.

Financial discipline is essential when bootstrapping. Creating a lean budget and sticking to it can make or break your business. List all your necessary expenses and prioritize them. Separate your needs from your wants. For instance, you need a functioning website, but you might not need a fancy office space right away. Regularly reviewing your financial statements is also critical. Set aside time each month to go over your income and expenses. This practice helps you identify areas where you can cut costs or invest more. Avoiding unnecessary expenses is vital. It's tempting to splurge on the latest gadgets or office decor, but remember that every dollar saved can be reinvested into your business's growth.

Checklist: Practical Bootstrapping Tips

- Rent vs. Buy: Opt for renting equipment initially to save on costs.
- Low-Cost Tools: Use free or affordable software like Canva, Trello, and Wave.
- Negotiate Terms: Seek better deals with suppliers by committing to longer-term contracts.
- Set Aside Income: Save a portion of your salary specifically for business use.
- Reinvest Profits: Channel your initial earnings back into the business for faster growth.
- Lean Budget: Create a strict budget and prioritize essential expenses.
- Regular Reviews: Review your financial statements monthly to stay on track.
- Avoid Splurging: Resist the urge to spend on non-essential items.

Bootstrapping your startup may require sacrifices and a lot of hard work, but it gives you full control over your business. By minimizing costs, generating internal capital, and managing your finances wisely, you can build a strong foundation for your venture without relying on external funding. This approach not only keeps you in the driver's seat but also lays the groundwork for sustainable growth.

4.2 Exploring Angel Investors and Venture Capital

When you're ready to take your business to the next level, seeking external funding can provide the boost you need. Angel investors and venture capitalists are two common sources of such funding, each with distinct characteristics. Angel investors are typically affluent individuals who provide capital for startups in exchange for equity or convertible debt. They often invest their own money and may offer mentorship and guidance. Venture capitalists, on the other hand, are part of VC firms that pool money from various investors to fund startups. These firms usually focus on businesses with high growth potential and provide significant funding, often in multiple rounds.

The benefits of seeking external funding can be substantial. One of the primary advantages is the potential for rapid growth and scaling. With an influx of capital, you can hire more staff, develop new products, and expand your market reach much faster than bootstrapping alone. For instance, companies like Uber and Airbnb scaled rapidly due to substantial VC funding. However, bringing in outside investors means you'll lose some degree of control over your business. Investors will want a say in major decisions, and you may need to adjust your vision to align with their expectations. Additionally, there's often pressure to achieve quick returns. Investors are looking for a profitable exit, which can mean pushing for aggressive growth strategies that may not always align with your long-term goals. It's important to recognize that external financiers have accumulated their wealth through astute business growth strategies. Their insights are often invaluable and can significantly contribute to elevating your business to the next level.

Attracting angel investors and venture capitalists requires a compelling pitch. Start by crafting a pitch deck that tells your story succinctly and engagingly. This deck should cover essential aspects like your business model, market opportunity, competitive landscape, and financial projections. Highlighting your unique value proposition is crucial. Explain what sets your business apart and why it's poised for success. For example, if you're developing a new app, emphasize its unique features and the specific problem it solves. Showcasing market potential with data and trends can also make your pitch more compelling. Investors want to see that there's a significant demand for your product or service.

Building a solid team is another key factor. Investors bet on people as much as they do on ideas. A strong, experienced team can inspire confidence and demonstrate that your business has the expertise needed to succeed. Highlight the backgrounds and achievements of your core team members in your pitch. If you have advisors or mentors with relevant industry experience, mention them as well. Their involvement can add credibility to your venture.

When you catch the interest of investors, the process moves into due diligence. This is where investors scrutinize every aspect of your business to assess its viability. They'll examine your financial statements, business model, market research, and legal documents. Be prepared to answer detailed questions and provide thorough documentation. Transparency is crucial during this phase. Investors want to ensure there are no hidden issues that could jeopardize their investment.

Negotiating terms and valuations is the next step. This can be a delicate process, as you'll need to agree on how much of your company the investors will own in exchange for their capital. Understanding equity dilution is vital here. Equity dilution occurs when new shares are issued, reducing the ownership percentage of existing shareholders. For example, if you own 100% of your business and bring in an investor who takes a 20% stake, your ownership drops to 80%. While dilution is a natural part of raising capital, it's important to strike a balance between attracting investment and maintaining control.

Throughout this process, remember that investors are looking for a return on their investment. They'll want to know your exit strategy—how and when they can expect to see a return. This could be through an Initial Public Offering (IPO), acquisition, or buyback. Clearly outlining your exit strategy can make your business more attractive to investors.

Navigating the world of angel investors and venture capitalists can be complex, but it offers the potential for significant growth and success. By crafting a compelling pitch, building a strong team, and understanding the investment process, you can attract the funding needed to take your business to new heights.

4.3 Leveraging Crowdfunding Platforms

Crowdfunding has revolutionized the way entrepreneurs can raise money for their projects. It's a method where you gather small amounts of capital from a large number of people, usually via the internet. This approach democratizes fundraising, allowing anyone with a compelling idea to seek financial support. There are three main types of crowdfunding: reward-based, equity-based, and donation-based. In reward-based crowdfunding, backers contribute money in exchange for a reward, such as a product or service, once your project is completed. Equity-based crowdfunding involves offering a stake in your business in return for investment, much like angel investing but on a broader scale. Donation-based crowdfunding is more philanthropic, where people contribute without expecting anything in return, often seen in charitable projects. While my own ventures developed prior to the advent of crowdfunding, making me inexperienced with this method firsthand, its potential and success stories in the modern business landscape cannot be overstated.

There are many advantages to crowdfunding. One of the most significant benefits is market validation. When people are willing to put their money behind your idea, it's a strong indicator that there's demand for your product or service. Crowdfunding also helps build a community around your brand. Your backers become your first customers and evangelists, spreading the word and creating buzz. However, crowdfunding isn't without its challenges. Managing a campaign can be time-consuming and demanding. You have to keep backers updated, manage rewards, and ensure the campaign stays on track. There's also the risk of not reaching your funding goals, which can be discouraging and potentially tarnish your brand's reputation.

Creating a successful crowdfunding campaign requires careful planning and execution. Start by setting realistic funding goals. Research similar projects to gauge what's achievable and ensure your goal is sufficient to bring your idea to life. Crafting a compelling story is crucial. People back projects they connect with emotionally. Share your journey, the problem you're solving, and how your product or service will make a difference. A well-made pitch video can significantly boost your campaign's appeal. Keep it concise, engaging, and professional. Show the product in action, introduce yourself and your team, and explain why you need support. Offering attractive rewards is key to enticing backers. Think about what would excite your audience—early bird specials, exclusive products, or personalized experiences.

Promoting your campaign is equally important. Leverage social media to spread the word. Create a content calendar to keep your audience engaged with regular updates, behind-the-scenes looks, and countdowns. Reach out to influencers and bloggers who might be interested in your project. Email marketing can also be effective. Build a list of potential backers and keep them informed before and during your campaign. It's all about creating momentum and maintaining it throughout the campaign period.

There are numerous examples of successful crowdfunding campaigns that can serve as inspiration. The Exploding Kittens card game raised over $8 million on Kickstarter. Their success was due to a combination of a unique concept, strategic rewards, and effective social media engagement. Another example is the Pebble Time smartwatch, which raised over $20 million on Kickstarter. Their clear messaging and compelling video content played a significant role in attracting backers. Both campaigns had a strong narrative, well-defined goals, and robust promotional strategies, which are essential elements for any successful crowdfunding effort.

Crowdfunding can be a powerful tool for funding your business. By understanding its different types, weighing the pros and cons, and following a structured approach to planning and executing your campaign, you can harness the power of the crowd to bring your entrepreneurial dreams to life.

4.4 Small Business Loans and Grants

Finding the right funding for your business can feel like navigating a maze, but understanding the different types of small business loans available can simplify the process. Term loans are one of the most common options. These loans provide a lump sum of money that you repay over a fixed period, usually with a fixed interest rate. They are great for significant one-time investments, like purchasing equipment or expanding your operations. The Small Business Administration (SBA) offers various loan programs designed to support small businesses. SBA loans are popular because they come with favorable terms and lower interest rates, thanks to the SBA guaranteeing a portion of the loan. This reduces the risk for lenders and makes it easier for you to secure the funding. This approach was instrumental in the expansion of my own enterprises. However, a word of caution—my initial foray into business ended in bankruptcy, primarily due to an inability to keep up with the bank's repayment demands. In subsequent ventures, I was mindful of this risk, ensuring it never posed a problem again.

Microloans are another option, especially if you need a smaller amount of capital. These loans, often provided by nonprofit organizations, typically range up to $50,000 and can be used for working capital, inventory, or equipment. The SBA also backs microloans, making them a reliable choice for new entrepreneurs. Equipment financing is a specialized loan used to purchase business equipment. The equipment itself serves as collateral, which can make it easier to qualify for this type of loan. It's an excellent option if your business relies heavily on machinery or technology that requires significant upfront investment.

Taking out a loan has its benefits and drawbacks. On the plus side, loans provide immediate capital, allowing you to make necessary investments without waiting to save up funds. There are also tax advantages, as the interest paid on business loans is usually tax-deductible. However, loans come with the obligation to repay the borrowed amount plus interest, which can strain your cash flow, especially if your business experiences fluctuations in revenue. Additionally, failing to meet repayment terms can harm your credit score and jeopardize your business's future.

Applying for a small business loan requires preparation and attention to detail. Start by preparing a solid business plan and financial statements. Lenders want to see that you have a clear vision for your business and a strategy for achieving your goals. Your business plan should include detailed financial projections, demonstrating your ability to repay the loan. Next, ensure you meet the credit requirements. Lenders typically look at your personal and business credit scores, so it's essential to maintain good credit. If your credit isn't strong, consider taking steps to improve it before applying.

Approaching banks and online lenders is the next step. Traditional banks offer a range of loan products, but the application process can be rigorous and time-consuming. Online lenders, on the other hand, often provide faster approval and more flexible terms, though they may come with higher interest rates. Research different lenders to find the one that best fits your needs. When you're ready to apply, gather all necessary documentation, including your business plan, financial statements, tax returns, and any other supporting materials. Submit your application and be prepared to discuss your business in detail during the review process.

Securing business grants is another avenue for funding, offering the advantage of non-repayable funds. Grants are typically provided by government agencies, foundations, and corporations to support specific industries or initiatives. Identifying relevant grants for your business requires research. Start by exploring databases like Grants.gov, which lists federal grants, or visit the websites of industry-specific organizations that offer grants.

Writing a compelling grant proposal is crucial for success. Your proposal should clearly outline your business's goals, the problem you're addressing, and how the grant funds will help you achieve your objectives. Be specific and provide detailed plans and budgets. Meeting eligibility criteria and reporting requirements is also essential. Each grant comes with specific qualifications, such as being a minority-owned business or operating in a particular industry. Ensure you meet all criteria before applying. Once you receive a grant, you'll need to report on how the funds are used, demonstrating that you've met the grant's requirements.

Navigating the world of small business loans and grants can be challenging, but understanding your options and preparing thoroughly can increase your chances of securing the funding you need. Whether you choose a loan or a grant, the right financial support can provide the boost your business needs to thrive and grow. In the next chapter, we'll explore additional strategies to ensure your business operations run smoothly and efficiently.

Chapter 5

Setting Up Your Operations

To ensure the seamless operation of your business, careful planning is necessary in several key areas:

- Choosing Appropriate Digital Tools
- Guidelines: Effective Implementation of Digital Tools
- Establishing a Productive Home Office or Workspace
- Guidelines: Essential Items for Your Home Office
- Adopting Efficient Time Management Techniques
- Cultivating a Robust Support Network

When I first launched my business, I was juggling countless tasks. From managing client relationships to ensuring timely deliveries, it felt like I was constantly putting out fires. It became clear that to truly succeed, I needed more than just hard work. I needed the right tools to streamline operations and boost productivity. Before the advent of today's online tools, I navigated my business operations without the digital aids available now. Welcome to the digital age, where technology can be your best ally in running a smooth and efficient business. For early retirees seeking a new venture, empty-nesters looking to fill their time productively, or the younger generation keen on carving a path outside the corporate world, embracing digital tools in your business operations can significantly elevate your entrepreneurial journey.

5.1 Selecting the Right Digital Tools

Digital tools have revolutionized how businesses operate. They enhance efficiency, productivity, and scalability, allowing you to focus on what truly matters—growing your business. Imagine managing your tasks, communicating with your team, and tracking your finances all from one place. Digital tools make this possible. For instance, when I integrated digital tools into my business, I saw a significant improvement in productivity. Tasks that once took hours were completed in minutes. Communication became seamless, and financial tracking was more accurate and less time-consuming. The result? A more efficient operation and a happier, more productive team.

Let's look at some real-world examples. Trello, a project management tool, helped a small marketing agency streamline its project workflows. Before Trello, the team struggled with keeping track of tasks and deadlines. After integrating Trello, they saw a 30% increase in project completion rates. Slack, a communication tool, transformed how a tech startup communicated internally. They moved from chaotic email threads to organized channels, improving team collaboration and reducing email clutter by 50%. QuickBooks, a financial tracking tool, enabled a retail business to manage its finances more effectively. They reduced the time spent on bookkeeping by 40%, allowing them to focus more on strategic growth. Incorporating QuickBooks into my operations streamlined my financial recording to such an extent that it led to a significant reduction in overhead costs. Not only was I able to manage without a dedicated accountant, but the streamlined, digital format also prompted my tax preparer to lower his fees, thanks to the ease with which he could now process my business's financial data into his software.

Statistics support the effectiveness of these tools. According to a study by McKinsey, companies that use digital tools for project management see a 20-25% increase in productivity. Another study by the Harvard Business Review found that businesses using digital communication tools like Slack experience a 32% improvement in team collaboration. These numbers highlight the tangible benefits of integrating digital tools into your operations.

So, what tools should you consider for your business? For project management, Trello and Asana are excellent choices. Trello offers a visual approach to task management with boards, lists, and cards, making it easy to track the progress of projects. Asana, on the other hand, provides more detailed task management features, including timelines and workload tracking. For communication, Slack and Zoom are indispensable. Slack offers real-time messaging, easily organized by channels, while Zoom provides robust video conferencing capabilities, perfect for remote team meetings. For financial tracking, QuickBooks and Xero are highly recommended. QuickBooks is user-friendly and offers comprehensive features for managing invoices, expenses, and payroll. Xero provides similar functionalities with a focus on real-time financial data and seamless integration with other business tools.

Choosing the right tools involves considering several criteria. First, ease of use is crucial. The tools should be intuitive and easy to adopt. After all, a tool is only effective if your team can use it without extensive training. Scalability is another important factor. As your business grows, your tools should be able to grow with you. Look for tools that offer flexible plans and can handle increased workloads. Integration capabilities are essential. The tools you choose should work well together, allowing for seamless data exchange and reducing the need for manual data entry. Cost-effectiveness is also key. While some tools are free, others come with a price tag. Assess your budget and choose tools that offer the best value for your investment.

Implementing digital tools successfully requires a strategic approach. Start by conducting team training sessions. Ensure everyone understands how to use the tools and their benefits. Interactive workshops or online tutorials can be very effective. Setting up user guides and resources can also help. These can be simple documents or videos that team members can refer to as needed. Regularly reviewing tool effectiveness is crucial. Schedule periodic check-ins to assess how well the tools are meeting your needs. Gather feedback from your team and make adjustments as necessary. This iterative process ensures you get the most out of your digital tools and can adapt to changing requirements.

5.2 Checklist: Tips for Implementing Digital Tools

- Team Training Sessions: Conduct interactive workshops or online tutorials.
- User Guides and Resources: Create easy-to-follow documents or videos.
- Regular Reviews: Schedule periodic check-ins to assess tool effectiveness.
- Gather Feedback: Listen to your team and make necessary adjustments.

Incorporating digital tools into your business operations can significantly enhance efficiency, productivity, and scalability. By choosing the right tools, training your team, and regularly reviewing their effectiveness, you can streamline your processes and focus on what truly matters—growing your business and achieving your entrepreneurial goals.

5.3 Setting Up Your Home Office or Workspace

Creating a dedicated workspace can significantly impact your productivity and work-life balance. It's not just about having a spot to place your laptop; it's about creating an environment where you can focus and thrive. When I first started working from home, I realized that the kitchen table wasn't cutting it. so I created a space in a den dedicated to my business. I needed a space that was solely dedicated to work, free from the distractions of daily life. A well-designed workspace not only boosts your efficiency but also helps you mentally switch between work and relaxation. Entrepreneurs like Sara Blakely, the founder of Spanx, have credited their home offices for boosting their productivity. Sara created a dedicated space that allowed her to focus entirely on her business without the usual home distractions.

Choosing the ideal location for your home office is crucial. You want a spot that minimizes distractions and maximizes efficiency. Natural light can be a game-changer. It not only brightens up the space but also has a positive effect on your mood and energy levels. If possible, set up your workspace near a window. Ventilation is equally important. A well-ventilated room prevents stuffiness and keeps you alert. Make sure your office is in a quiet part of the house, away from household activities. This helps you concentrate and reduces interruptions. When I moved my workspace to the spare bedroom, the difference was night and day. It was quieter, brighter, and far more conducive to getting work done.

Equipping your workspace with the right furniture and equipment can make all the difference. Start with an ergonomic chair and desk. You'll spend hours sitting, so comfort is paramount. An ergonomic chair supports your posture, reducing the risk of back pain. Similarly, an adjustable desk lets you switch between sitting and standing, which is great for your health. Invest in a high-quality computer and monitor. A reliable computer ensures you can run all necessary applications smoothly, while a high-resolution monitor reduces eye strain. Don't skimp on your internet connection either. A fast and stable connection is vital for video calls, online research, and cloud-based applications. Storage solutions are another key component. Shelves, filing cabinets, and desk organizers help keep your workspace tidy and clutter-free, which in turn helps you stay focused.

Designing an inspiring and functional workspace is also about aesthetics. The colors you choose can influence your mood and productivity. For instance, blue is known to boost focus and efficiency, while green has a calming effect. Incorporating plants can bring a touch of nature to your workspace, improving air quality and reducing stress. Personalizing your space with motivating decor can also make a big difference. Whether it's a vision board, inspirational quotes, or photos of loved ones, these personal touches can boost your morale and keep you motivated. I found that adding a few plants and some art pieces transformed my workspace into a place I actually enjoyed spending time in.

5.4 Checklist: Home Office Essentials

- Ergonomic Chair and Desk: Ensures comfort and supports good posture.
- High-Quality Computer and Monitor: Essential for smooth operations and reduced eye strain.
- Reliable Internet Connection: Vital for seamless online activities.
- Storage Solutions: Keeps your workspace organized and clutter-free.
- Natural Light and Ventilation: Enhances mood and productivity.
- Quiet Environment: Minimizes distractions and interruptions.
- Inspiring Decor: Boosts morale and personalizes your space.

When setting up your home office, consider these tips to create an environment that enhances productivity and supports your well-being. A well-thought-out workspace can be a sanctuary where you focus, create, and build your business without the usual distractions of home life. By investing time and effort into setting up your workspace, you set the stage for success and make working from home a more enjoyable and effective experience.

5.5 Implementing Effective Time Management Strategies

Time management is one of those skills that can make or break your entrepreneurial efforts. When I first started my own business, I quickly realized that if I didn't manage my time well, I'd end up overwhelmed and stressed, which would undoubtedly affect my productivity. Entrepreneurs who master time management often find themselves not just surviving but thriving. Take Richard Branson, for example. He attributes much of his success to his ability to manage time effectively, allowing him to juggle multiple ventures seamlessly. According to a study by McKinsey, executives who effectively manage their time are 25% more productive. That's a significant increase, and it's achievable with the right strategies.

One of the most effective techniques for prioritizing tasks is using the Eisenhower Matrix. This method categorizes tasks into four quadrants: urgent and important, important but not urgent, urgent but not important, and neither urgent nor important. This helps you focus on what truly matters and avoid getting bogged down by trivial tasks. Another powerful technique is time-blocking. By allocating specific blocks of time to different activities, you can ensure that each task gets the attention it deserves. For instance, dedicating a block of time each morning to answering emails can prevent them from distracting you throughout the day.

The Pomodoro Technique is another time management tool that can boost productivity. This method involves working in focused intervals, typically 25 minutes, followed by a short break. After four intervals, you take a longer break. This approach keeps your mind fresh and helps maintain focus. Setting SMART goals for daily tasks can also be incredibly effective. By making your goals Specific, Measurable, Achievable, Relevant, and Time-bound, you give yourself clear targets to aim for each day. For example, instead of saying, "I'll work on marketing today," a SMART goal would be, "I'll create and schedule five social media posts by 3 PM."

Digital tools can further enhance your time management efforts. Time-tracking apps like Toggl and Harvest allow you to monitor how you spend your time, helping you identify areas for improvement. These apps can break down your day into categories, showing you exactly where your time goes. Task management apps like Todoist and Microsoft To-Do can keep you organized by allowing you to create to-do lists, set deadlines, and prioritize tasks. Calendar apps like Google Calendar and Apple Calendar help you plan your day efficiently. You can schedule meetings, set reminders, and even share your calendar with your team to ensure everyone is on the same page.

Balancing work and personal life is crucial for maintaining long-term productivity and well-being. One effective strategy is setting clear boundaries between work and personal time. Designate specific work hours and stick to them. When work time is over, allow yourself to disconnect and focus on personal activities. Scheduling regular breaks and leisure activities can also help. Short breaks throughout the day can rejuvenate your mind, while longer breaks or vacations can prevent burnout. Practicing mindfulness and stress-relief techniques, such as meditation or deep-breathing exercises, can help you stay calm and focused. Apps like Headspace or Calm offer guided sessions that can fit into a busy schedule.

Effective time management is about more than just getting things done. It's about creating a balanced life where you can be productive without sacrificing your well-being. By prioritizing tasks, using digital tools, and maintaining a healthy work-life balance, you can set yourself up for success. This approach not only boosts productivity but also reduces stress, making your entrepreneurial journey more enjoyable and sustainable.

5.6 Building a Strong Support Network

When I first ventured into entrepreneurship, I quickly realized that going it alone was not an option. A strong support network is invaluable—it provides guidance, motivation, and resources that can make all the difference. Imagine navigating the complexities of starting a business without anyone to turn to for advice or support. It's daunting. Entrepreneurs like Steve Jobs and Oprah Winfrey credit much of their success to their mentors and support networks. Jobs had Mike Markkula, an early investor and advisor at Apple, while Winfrey had Maya Angelou, who provided wisdom and encouragement. These relationships were crucial in helping them navigate challenges and seize opportunities.

Mentors can be a game-changer. They offer insights from their own experiences, helping you avoid common pitfalls and make informed decisions. Finding a mentor starts with putting yourself in the right places. Attend industry events and networking sessions where experienced professionals gather. These events are fertile ground for making connections. Join professional associations and online communities related to your field. These groups often have mentorship programs or at least provide opportunities to meet potential mentors. Don't underestimate the power of social media platforms like LinkedIn. Reach out to professionals whose careers you admire. A thoughtful message expressing your admiration and interest in their work can open doors to valuable relationships.

Entrepreneurial communities offer a different but equally important kind of support. Being part of a community provides access to resources, collaboration opportunities, and a sense of belonging.

Communities like Startup Grind and Founders Network are excellent for connecting with fellow entrepreneurs, sharing experiences, and finding potential collaborators. Online forums and groups such as those on Reddit or Facebook can also be incredibly valuable. These platforms allow you to tap into a global network of entrepreneurs, providing diverse perspectives and solutions to common challenges. Engaging with these communities can offer you the encouragement and practical advice you need to keep pushing forward.

Maintaining and nurturing your support network requires effort and reciprocity. Regular check-ins and updates are essential. Don't wait for crises to reach out. Keep your mentors and peers informed about your progress and challenges. This keeps the relationship active and allows for timely advice. Offering value in return is crucial. Whether it's sharing your own insights, providing introductions, or offering help with their projects, reciprocity strengthens your connections. Participating in community events and discussions also keeps you engaged and visible. Attend meetups, webinars, and forums to contribute and learn. These interactions reinforce your presence in the community and build stronger bonds.

In the early days of one of my ventures, I found myself struggling with a particularly challenging marketing strategy. I reached out to a mentor I had met at a networking event, and their advice was pivotal. They not only provided strategic insights but also connected me with a marketing expert who helped refine our approach. This experience reinforced the importance of having a robust support network. It's not just about getting advice; it's about having access to a wealth of knowledge and resources that can help you overcome hurdles and achieve your goals.

Building a strong support network is an ongoing process. It's about cultivating relationships that offer mutual benefits and maintaining those connections through regular engagement. Whether it's mentors who provide guidance or peer groups that offer camaraderie and collaboration, your support network is a vital component of your entrepreneurial success. By investing time and effort into building and nurturing these relationships, you create a safety net that not only helps you navigate challenges but also propels you toward your goals.

Chapter 6
Marketing Your Business

For a business to flourish, it's crucial that potential customers can discover it effortlessly. This underscores the pivotal role of marketing, which encompasses:

- Cultivating Your Brand Identity
- Conducting a Brand Audit
- Formulating a Digital Marketing Plan
- Harnessing social media to Propel Business Expansion
- Capitalizing on Content Marketing

When I first stepped into the world of entrepreneurship, I quickly realized that having a great product or service was only half the battle. The other half? Marketing. How do you make people notice you in a crowded marketplace? How do you build a brand that people recognize and trust? These questions can be daunting, especially if you're transitioning from a corporate job, retiring early, or exploring a second career. But here's the good news: marketing is not as mystifying as it seems. With the right strategies, you can create a brand that stands out and connects with your audience.

6.1 Developing Your Brand Identity

Brand identity is the face of your business. It's more than just a logo or a catchy tagline; it's the entire experience people have with your brand. According to TopNotchDezigns, brand identity encompasses all tangible elements used to portray your business, including logos, website design, and digital marketing materials. It helps create a unique position in the market, builds a loyal customer base, and visually depicts your business's values.

At the core of brand identity are several key components. First, there's the logo. This is often the first thing people see and is a symbol that represents your business. Think about the iconic swoosh of Nike or the bitten apple of Apple. These logos are instantly recognizable and convey a sense of trust and quality. Alongside the logo is the color palette. Colors evoke emotions and can influence how people perceive your brand. For instance, blue often conveys trust and professionalism, while red can evoke excitement and urgency. Typography, or the fonts you use, also plays a crucial role. It should reflect your brand's personality—whether it's playful, elegant, or professional. Finally, there's the brand voice. This is how you communicate with your audience, whether through social media posts, customer service interactions, or marketing campaigns. A consistent brand voice builds familiarity and trust.

Creating a unique and memorable brand identity starts with a brand audit. This involves evaluating your current brand elements and understanding how they're perceived by your audience. Ask for feedback from customers, conduct surveys, and review your online presence. This will give you a clear picture of your starting point. Next, define your brand values and mission. What does your business stand for? What are your core principles? Your values and mission should guide all your branding efforts, ensuring they align with your overall goals.

Once you have a clear understanding of your current brand and its values, it's time to bring it all together. Consistency is key. Consistent branding across all platforms builds trust and recognition. Develop brand guidelines that outline how your logo should be used, what colors and fonts are acceptable, and the tone of your brand voice. For example, Apple's branding is consistent across all its marketing materials, from its website to its product packaging. This uniformity ensures that every interaction with the brand feels cohesive and professional.

But what if your brand identity no longer aligns with your market or values? A rebrand might be necessary. Rebranding is a significant step that involves changing your logo, color palette, typography, and even your brand voice. Start with thorough research to understand what needs to change and why. Design new brand elements that reflect your updated values and mission. Finally, implement the rebrand across all platforms, from your website to your social media profiles. Successful rebrands include Old Spice, which transformed its image from an old-fashioned brand to a modern, edgy one, and Burberry, which revitalized its brand to appeal to a younger, more fashion-forward audience.

6.2 Exercise: Brand Audit

Take some time to conduct a brand audit. Reflect on your current brand elements and gather feedback from your customers. Use the questions below to guide your audit:

1) How do customers currently perceive your brand?
2) What emotions do your logo, colors, and typography evoke?
3) Are your brand values and mission clearly communicated?
4) Is your brand voice consistent across all platforms?

Brand identity is crucial for business success. It helps differentiate you from competitors, builds trust with your audience, and creates a memorable experience. By focusing on key components like logo, color palette, typography, and brand voice, and ensuring consistency across all platforms, you can develop a strong and cohesive brand identity. If necessary, a well-executed rebrand can align your business with your current market and values, ensuring continued growth and success.

6.3 Crafting a Digital Marketing Strategy

Creating a digital marketing strategy is crucial for driving business growth and engaging your customers. In today's digital age, a well-crafted strategy can significantly boost your visibility and sales. Statistics show that businesses with robust digital marketing strategies see higher engagement and conversion rates. According to the Digital Marketing Institute, companies that excel in digital marketing generate 78% more revenue than those that do not. For instance, a small bakery that used targeted online ads and email campaigns increased its sales by 30% within six months. A solid digital marketing strategy can transform your business, making it more competitive and resilient.

Setting digital marketing goals is the first step in crafting your strategy. Clear, measurable objectives guide your efforts and help you track progress. Start by setting SMART goals—Specific, Measurable, Achievable, Relevant, and Time-bound. For example, instead of saying, "I want more website traffic," a SMART goal would be, "I aim to increase website traffic by 20% over the next three months by optimizing SEO and running targeted ads." Another example might be, "Grow my email list by 15% within two months by offering a free eBook in exchange for sign-ups." These goals give you a clear target and a way to measure success, ensuring your efforts are focused and effective.

A comprehensive digital marketing strategy includes several key components. Search Engine Optimization (SEO) is essential for improving your website's visibility on search engines like Google. By optimizing your content and using relevant keywords, you can attract more organic traffic. Pay-Per-Click (PPC) advertising is another powerful tool. It allows you to place ads on search engines and social media, paying only when someone clicks on your ad. This can drive immediate traffic to your site and generate leads. Email marketing remains one of the most effective ways to engage with your audience. Regular newsletters, promotional offers, and personalized content can keep your subscribers engaged and loyal. Social media marketing is also vital. Platforms like Facebook, Instagram, and LinkedIn offer opportunities to connect with your audience, build relationships, and promote your products or services.

To create a digital marketing plan, start with a digital audit. Assess your current online presence by reviewing your website, social media profiles, and any existing digital marketing efforts. Identify what's working and what needs improvement. Next, create buyer personas to understand your target audience better. These personas should include demographic information, interests, pain points, and online behavior. For instance, if you're targeting young professionals, your persona might include details like age range, job titles, and preferred social media platforms. Developing a content calendar is the next step. Plan and schedule your content in advance, ensuring a consistent and strategic approach. This could include blog posts, social media updates, email newsletters, and more.

Visual elements like infographics can make your content more engaging and shareable. Interactive elements such as quizzes or polls can increase engagement and provide valuable insights into your audience's preferences. Case studies can showcase your success stories, providing social proof and building trust with potential customers. Regularly reviewing your analytics is crucial. Tools like Google Analytics can help you track your website traffic, understand user behavior, and measure the effectiveness of your marketing efforts. Adjust your strategy based on these insights to optimize your performance continually.

A digital marketing strategy is not a one-time effort but an ongoing process. It requires regular monitoring, analysis, and adjustments to stay relevant and effective. By setting clear goals, understanding your audience, and leveraging various digital marketing components, you can create a strategy that drives growth and engagement. Whether you're an early retiree looking to start a new venture, an empty-nester seeking a fulfilling second career, or a young professional eager to explore entrepreneurship, a strong digital marketing strategy can help you achieve your business goals.

6.4 Utilizing Social Media for Business Growth

Social media has revolutionized how businesses market themselves. It's no longer just about broadcasting messages; it's about creating interactions and building relationships. Social media platforms play a crucial role in enhancing brand visibility and engaging with customers. Statistics show that social media usage is at an all-time high, with US adults spending an average of 2.25 hours daily on these platforms. Businesses that leverage social media effectively see increased brand awareness, higher customer engagement, and, ultimately, better sales. For example, small businesses like Glossier and Warby Parker have successfully used social media to build loyal customer bases and drive sales.

Choosing the right social media platforms is critical for your business. Each platform has its unique strengths and audience demographics. Facebook, for instance, is ideal for reaching a broad audience and building community relationships. It's perfect for sharing updates, hosting events, and engaging with customers through comments and messages. Instagram, on the other hand, is visually driven and great for brands that can leverage photos and videos. It's particularly popular among younger audiences and is excellent for influencer partnerships. LinkedIn is the go-to platform for B2B companies and professionals. It's ideal for sharing industry insights, connecting with other businesses, and recruiting talent. Twitter excels in real-time updates and customer service, while TikTok is rapidly gaining popularity for its short, engaging videos that resonate with a younger demographic. When choosing platforms, consider your target audience's age, interests, and online behavior.

Creating engaging social media content is both an art and a science. It's not just about posting regularly; it's about posting content that resonates with your audience. Videos are highly effective, as they capture attention quickly and can convey a lot of information in a short time. Whether it's a behind-the-scenes look at your business, a product demo, or a customer testimonial, videos can significantly boost engagement. Infographics are another powerful tool. They present information visually, making it easier to digest and share. User-generated content, such as customer reviews and photos, can build trust and authenticity. Encourage your customers to share their experiences with your products and feature their content on your social media pages. Storytelling is also essential. Share stories about your brand's journey, your team, and your customers. Use visuals to enhance your stories, making them more appealing and memorable.

Managing your social media efficiently is crucial for maintaining a consistent and professional presence. Tools like Hootsuite, Buffer, and Sprout Social can help you schedule posts, track performance, and engage with your audience. These tools allow you to plan your content calendar, ensuring you always have fresh content ready to go. They also provide analytics, helping you understand what's working and what's not. For instance, Hootsuite offers detailed reports on engagement metrics, such as likes, comments, and shares. Buffer allows you to schedule posts across multiple platforms and provides insights into the best times to post. Sprout Social combines social media management with powerful analytics, offering a comprehensive solution for businesses.

Scheduling posts is a game-changer. It allows you to maintain a steady flow of content without the stress of daily posting. Batch-create your content and schedule it in advance. This approach frees up time to engage with your audience and focus on other aspects of your business. Tracking metrics is equally important. Pay attention to key performance indicators (KPIs) such as engagement rate, reach, and conversions. These metrics give you valuable insights into your social media performance and help you refine your strategy. Use the data to experiment with different types of content, posting times, and engagement techniques.

Social media is a powerful tool for business growth. By choosing the right platforms, creating engaging content, and using management tools, you can enhance your brand's visibility and build strong relationships with your customers. Whether you're an early retiree, an empty-nester, or a young professional, mastering social media marketing can significantly impact your business's success.

6.5 Leveraging Content Marketing

Content marketing is a strategy focused on creating and distributing valuable, relevant, and consistent content to attract and engage a clearly defined audience. It's about offering something of value to your customers—something that informs, entertains, or solves a problem for them. This type of marketing can drive customer engagement and business growth in several ways. For instance, it can increase website traffic by drawing in visitors who are interested in your content. It also helps in building brand authority, as consistently high-quality content positions you as an expert in your field. Additionally, content marketing can improve customer retention by keeping your audience engaged and coming back for more.

Consider the success of HubSpot, a company that has built a massive following through its content marketing efforts. HubSpot offers a wealth of resources, including blog posts, eBooks, and webinars, all aimed at helping businesses improve their marketing, sales, and customer service. This content not only attracts potential customers but also builds trust and establishes HubSpot as a leader in the industry. Another great example is Red Bull. Their content marketing strategy includes producing high-energy videos, articles, and events that align with their brand's adventurous spirit. This content keeps their audience engaged and loyal, ultimately driving sales.

Creating a content marketing strategy involves several key steps. Start by identifying your target audience and understanding their content preferences. What are their pain points? What type of content do they consume? Use this information to tailor your content to meet their needs and interests. Next, set clear content marketing goals and key performance indicators (KPIs). These could include increasing website traffic, boosting social media engagement, or growing your email list. Having specific goals helps you measure the success of your efforts and make necessary adjustments.

The types of content you include in your strategy should be diverse and cater to different segments of your audience. Blog posts and articles are great for providing detailed information and improving your search engine rankings. Whitepapers can offer in-depth insights and are particularly useful for B2B marketing. Videos are highly engaging and can be used for tutorials, product demos, or customer testimonials. Podcasts and webinars provide a platform for more in-depth discussions and can establish you as a thought leader in your industry. Infographics are excellent for presenting complex information in a visually appealing way. Case studies showcase your successes and offer social proof, while eBooks can provide comprehensive guides on relevant topics.

Distributing and promoting your content effectively is crucial for reaching the right audience. Social media is a powerful tool for sharing content and engaging with your audience. Platforms like Facebook, Twitter, and LinkedIn allow you to reach a broad audience and encourage interaction. Email marketing campaigns are another effective way to distribute content. Send regular newsletters featuring your latest blog posts, upcoming webinars, and exclusive resources. Collaborating with influencers and industry partners can also extend your reach. Influencers can share your content with their followers, while partnerships with industry leaders can lend credibility to your brand.

Using a mix of these strategies ensures that your content reaches a wide audience and keeps them engaged. Regularly monitor your analytics to see what's working and what's not. Adjust your strategy based on these insights to continually improve your content marketing efforts. Whether you're just starting out or looking to expand your business, a well-crafted content marketing strategy can help you connect with your audience, build trust, and drive growth. It's about delivering value consistently and creating a loyal following that supports your business goals.

Chapter 7
Sales Strategies

Exploring Strategies to Enhance
Our Marketing Initiatives:

- Developing an Effective Sales Funnel
- Honing Networking Skills
- Cultivating Strong Customer Connections
- Establishing a Robust Customer Feedback Mechanism

When I first started my business journey, I was overwhelmed by the sheer number of tasks that lay ahead. The excitement of launching something new was quickly tempered by the realization that I needed a solid plan to attract and convert customers. As I navigated these early days, I discovered the power of a well-crafted sales funnel. Think of it as guiding potential customers through a series of stages, from the moment they hear about your business to the point where they make a purchase. The sales funnel is your roadmap, ensuring you don't lose potential customers along the way.

7.1 Creating a Sales Funnel

A sales funnel represents the journey your customers take from becoming aware of your product or service to making a purchase. Visualized as a funnel, it starts wide at the top, capturing a broad audience, and narrows down as prospects move closer to buying. Understanding and optimizing each stage of the funnel is crucial for guiding potential customers through the buying process. The main stages of a sales funnel are Awareness, Interest, Decision, and Action.

At the top of the funnel (TOFU), the Awareness stage is where potential customers first learn about your business. This is crucial because you need to cast a wide net to attract as many leads as possible. You can generate awareness through content marketing techniques like blog posts, webinars, and social media campaigns. For instance, creating informative blog posts that answer common questions in your industry can draw in curious readers. Webinars allow you to showcase your expertise and engage with a live audience. Social media campaigns, with engaging visuals and compelling messages, can spread the word about your brand far and wide. Another effective tactic is using lead magnets, such as free eBooks or trials. These offers provide value upfront, encouraging potential customers to give you their contact information in exchange.

Once you've captured interest, you move to the middle of the funnel (MOFU), the Interest and Decision stages. Here, the goal is to nurture these leads and keep them engaged. Email marketing is a powerful tool for this. Sending personalized content that speaks to their specific needs and pain points helps build a relationship. For example, if someone downloaded your eBook on financial planning, follow up with emails containing case studies of how your services have helped others achieve their financial goals. Educational resources like tutorials can also be valuable. These materials provide deeper insights into your product or service, helping potential customers understand how it can solve their problems. The key is to offer consistent value, keeping your business top of mind as they consider their options.

At the bottom of the funnel (BOFU), the Action stage is where you convert leads into paying customers. This is where you pull out all the stops to close the sale. Special offers and discounts can provide that final nudge. For instance, offering a limited-time discount can create a sense of urgency, encouraging prospects to act quickly. Customer testimonials and success stories are incredibly persuasive. They provide social proof, showing potential customers that others have had positive experiences with your product. Clear calls to action (CTAs) are essential. Whether it's "Buy Now," "Sign Up Today," or "Get Started," your CTA should be straightforward and easy to follow. Streamlining your checkout process is also crucial. Remove any unnecessary steps that could cause frustration and lead to abandonment. Make it as easy as possible for your customers to complete their purchase.

Consider the example of Netflix, which uses a seven-stage funnel starting with a 30-day free trial. This hooks potential customers by offering risk-free access to their streaming service. Throughout the trial period, Netflix sends personalized recommendations and reminders to keep users engaged. As the trial nears its end, they offer a simple, one-click subscription option, making it easy to convert trial users into paying customers. This seamless transition from free trial to paid subscription is a textbook example of an effective sales funnel.

Implementing a sales funnel requires continuous monitoring and optimization. Track key metrics like lead quality, conversion rates at each stage, and customer acquisition costs. Use this data to identify any bottlenecks and make necessary adjustments. For instance, if you notice a drop-off between the Interest and Decision stages, you might need to improve your follow-up emails or offer more compelling educational content. Regularly refining your funnel ensures it remains effective in guiding potential customers from awareness to action.

A well-designed sales funnel is essential for any business. It helps you attract, nurture, and convert leads systematically, ensuring that no potential customer slips through the cracks. By understanding each stage of the funnel and implementing strategies to optimize it, you can drive more sales and grow your business. Remember, the goal is to create a smooth, engaging journey that leads your customers to choose your product or service.

7.2 Mastering the Art of Networking

When I first started building my business, I quickly realized that networking was more than just a buzzword. It was a lifeline. Meeting the right people opened doors to new opportunities and partnerships that I never would have found on my own. Networking isn't just about handing out business cards; it's about building relationships that can lead to meaningful connections and collaborations. Take the example of Reid Hoffman, co-founder of LinkedIn. He leveraged his network to connect with investors and partners, which played a significant role in LinkedIn's growth. According to a study by the Oxford Economics, 78% of startups attribute their success to networking (SOURCE: https://www.acuitymd.com/blog/why-networking-in-sales-is-so-important-12-tips).

Building a network starts with putting yourself out there. Attending industry conferences and trade shows is a great way to meet people who share your interests. These events are filled with potential partners, mentors, and customers. Don't just stick to the sessions; mingle during breaks, join group discussions, and attend networking events in the evenings. Joining professional associations and online forums can also expand your network. Organizations like the Chamber of Commerce or industry-specific groups offer regular meet-ups and resources. Online forums like Reddit and LinkedIn groups provide platforms to share insights and ask questions, helping you connect with like-minded individuals.

One of the most important aspects of networking is the follow-up. It's easy to collect a stack of business cards, but the real value comes from maintaining those connections. After meeting someone, send a personalized follow-up email or message. Mention something specific from your conversation to jog their memory. For example, "It was great discussing digital marketing strategies with you at the conference. I'd love to continue our conversation over coffee next week." Scheduling regular check-ins and coffee meetings helps keep the relationship alive. Set reminders to reach out every few months, even if it's just to say hello and share a quick update about your business. These small gestures can turn casual acquaintances into valuable connections over time.

In my most successful venture as a consultant, I embraced the power of networking by viewing fellow consultants not as competitors, but as collaborators. At various conferences, instead of guarding my knowledge, I shared insights and resources with them. This mutual exchange of information established a foundation of trust.

On occasions when a client's needs didn't align with my expertise or approach, I would recommend one of these trusted colleagues to take over the project. This approach ensured that the client's needs were better met, leaving them satisfied and well taken care of. Simultaneously, it strengthened my relationships with other consultants, who often reciprocated by referring clients to me. This cycle of goodwill and collaboration significantly contributed to the growth and success of my business.

Leveraging social media is another powerful way to expand your network. Platforms like LinkedIn are designed for professional networking. Start by optimizing your LinkedIn profile to attract connections. Use a professional photo, write a compelling headline, and fill out your profile with detailed information about your experience and skills. Join relevant groups and engage in discussions. Share industry insights and thought leadership content. For instance, if you're in the tech industry, share articles about the latest trends in AI or cybersecurity. Comment on posts, ask questions, and offer your expertise. This not only helps you connect with others but also establishes you as a knowledgeable professional in your field.

Quality networking isn't just about the number of connections you make; it's about the depth of those relationships. Be authentic and genuine in your interactions. People can sense when you're only interested in what they can do for you. Instead, focus on finding common ground and offering value. Maybe you can introduce them to someone in your network, share a useful resource, or offer advice on a challenge they're facing. Building rapport and trust takes time, but it's worth the effort. A strong network can provide support, advice, and opportunities that you wouldn't have access to otherwise.

One strategy that worked for me was setting clear networking goals. Before attending an event, I'd decide how many new connections I wanted to make or how many business cards I aimed to exchange. This gave me a target to work towards and made the experience more productive. I also made it a point to research the RSVP or guest list beforehand, identifying key individuals I wanted to connect with. This preparation helped me make the most of my time and ensured I met people who could genuinely benefit from my network.

Networking is a vital part of building a successful business. It opens doors, creates opportunities, and provides a support system that can help you navigate the challenges of entrepreneurship. By attending events, joining professional groups, following up diligently, and leveraging social media, you can build a network that supports and propels you forward. Remember, it's about building genuine relationships, not just collecting contacts. Invest the time and effort into nurturing your network, and it will pay dividends in ways you might not expect.

7.3 Building Customer Relationships

Building strong customer relationships is like laying the foundation for a sturdy house. Loyal customers are the backbone of sustained business growth. They not only provide consistent revenue but also promote your brand through word-of-mouth. Statistics show that acquiring a new customer can cost five times more than retaining an existing one. Moreover, increasing customer retention by just 5% can boost profits by 25% to 95%. Companies like Amazon and Apple have mastered customer loyalty, creating ecosystems where customers keep coming back, not just for the products, but for the experience and trust they offer.

Building trust and rapport with customers starts with personalized communication. Gone are the days of one-size-fits-all messaging. Today, customers expect businesses to understand their unique needs. Use CRM systems to gather data and personalize your interactions. For instance, if a customer frequently buys a specific type of product, send them personalized recommendations or exclusive discounts on similar items. Transparency and honesty in your dealings are also crucial. Be upfront about your policies, product limitations, and pricing. If something goes wrong, admit it and make it right. This honesty builds trust and shows customers that you value their business. Regular check-ins and follow-ups can make a significant difference. A simple email asking for feedback or a call to see how they're enjoying your product can go a long way in strengthening the relationship.

Excellent customer service is the linchpin of customer satisfaction and loyalty. When customers feel valued and heard, they are more likely to stay loyal and recommend your business to others. Train your employees to handle customer interactions professionally. Equip them with the knowledge and tools they need to resolve issues efficiently and empathetically. Implementing customer support systems like live chat and help desks can enhance the support experience. These systems allow customers to get immediate assistance, reducing frustration and increasing satisfaction. Consider the example of Zappos, known for its exceptional customer service. They empower their customer service representatives to go above and beyond, ensuring that every customer interaction is positive and memorable.

Creating a customer loyalty program can further cement these relationships, rewarding repeat business and encouraging referrals. There are various types of loyalty programs you can implement. Point-based programs, like Starbucks Rewards, allow customers to earn points for every purchase, which they can redeem for free products or discounts. Tiered programs, like Sephora's Beauty Insider, offer increasingly valuable perks as customers spend more, incentivizing higher spending. Referral programs reward customers for bringing in new business. For example, Dropbox offers extra storage space to users who refer friends. These programs not only reward loyalty but also turn your customers into advocates for your brand.

Starbucks Rewards is a shining example of a successful loyalty program. Customers earn "stars" for every purchase, which can be redeemed for free drinks, food, and merchandise. This program not only incentivizes repeat purchases but also provides Starbucks with valuable insights into customer behavior through their app. The North Face's XPLR Pass is another excellent example. Customers earn points not just for purchases but also for participating in events. These points can be redeemed for travel experiences, early access to products, and exclusive testing opportunities. Such programs create a sense of community and exclusivity, making customers feel like valued members of a club.

To develop your own loyalty program, start by understanding what your customers value most. Conduct surveys or focus groups to gather insights. Once you have a clear understanding, design a program that aligns with those values. Make it easy to join and participate, and ensure the rewards are meaningful and attainable. Promote your program through various channels, including your website, social media, and email marketing. Regularly review and adjust the program based on customer feedback and participation rates.

Strong customer relationships are the bedrock of a successful business. By building trust through personalized communication, transparency, and regular engagement, you can create lasting connections. Excellent customer service further enhances these relationships, while a well-designed loyalty program rewards and encourages repeat business. Investing in these strategies not only boosts customer retention but also turns your customers into passionate advocates for your brand.

7.4 Implementing a Customer Feedback Loop

Understanding what your customers think about your product or service is crucial. Their feedback can drive continuous improvement, helping you refine your offerings and stay ahead of the competition. Companies like Amazon and Apple have thrived by actively listening to their customers. Amazon's relentless focus on customer feedback has led to innovations like Prime and Alexa. According to a study by Microsoft, 77% of customers view brands more favorably if they proactively invite and accept customer feedback. This statistic underscores the significant impact that paying attention to your customers can have on your business success.

Collecting customer feedback is the first step in creating a feedback loop. There are several methods to gather valuable insights. Surveys and questionnaires are effective tools. You can send these out via email, include them on your website, or even integrate them into your product. For instance, after a purchase, you might ask customers to rate their experience and provide comments. Online reviews and social media comments are also gold mines for feedback. Platforms like Yelp, Google Reviews, and Facebook allow customers to share their thoughts publicly. Monitoring these channels can provide real-time insights into what people are saying about your business. Customer interviews and focus groups offer a more in-depth approach. These methods allow you to ask open-ended questions and dive deeper into specific issues or suggestions. For example, a focus group for a new product can reveal pain points that you might not have considered.

Once you've collected feedback, the next step is to analyze and act on it. Tools like sentiment analysis software can help you understand the overall mood of the feedback. These tools use algorithms to scan text and identify whether the sentiment is positive, negative, or neutral. For example, if you notice a trend of negative sentiments about your customer service, it's a clear indicator that changes are needed. Creating action plans based on feedback trends is essential. Start by categorizing

73

the feedback into themes, such as product features, customer service, or pricing. Then, prioritize the issues based on their impact and frequency. Develop specific action plans to address each issue. For instance, if multiple customers mention that your website is difficult to navigate, work on a redesign to improve user experience.

Closing the feedback loop is about showing your customers that you value their input and have acted on it. This step is often overlooked but is crucial for building trust and loyalty. Start by sending thank-you notes to customers who provided feedback. A simple message like "Thank you for your input. We're constantly looking to improve, and your feedback helps us do that" can go a long way. Update your customers on the changes you've made based on their feedback. For example, if you've added a new feature to your app based on user requests, highlight this improvement in your marketing materials. Use newsletters, blog posts, or social media updates to communicate these changes. This not only shows that you're listening but also encourages more customers to share their thoughts, knowing that their voices will be heard.

Let's look at a company that has successfully closed the feedback loop. Slack, the popular messaging app, regularly collects user feedback and uses it to make improvements. When they introduced the ability to customize notification settings based on user requests, they made sure to communicate this update widely. They sent out emails, posted on social media, and even included a notification within the app. This transparency not only improved user satisfaction but also reinforced the perception that Slack values its users' opinions.

Implementing a customer feedback loop involves actively seeking out feedback, analyzing it to identify trends, acting on it to make improvements, and then communicating those changes back to your customers. This process not only helps you improve your products and services but also builds stronger relationships with your customers. By showing that you value their input and are willing to make changes based on their suggestions, you foster a sense of loyalty and trust that can drive long-term success.

Chapter 8
Managing Finances

Securing initial funding was just the first step; ongoing financial management is crucial as your business evolves, covering key areas such as:

- Budgeting Essentials for Small Businesses
- A Checklist of Effective Budgeting Strategies
- Navigating Cash Flow Management
- Demystifying Financial Statements
- Implementing Cost-Reduction Tactics

When I first decided to leave the corporate world and start my own business, I quickly learned that managing finances was more than just keeping an eye on the cash flow. It was about planning, strategizing, and making informed decisions. Budgeting became the backbone of my financial strategy. The importance of a well-planned budget can't be overstated. It provides a roadmap for your financial goals, ensuring that you're not just making money but also managing it wisely. Effective budgeting helps you track revenue and expenses, meet financial goals, and prepare for unforeseen circumstances.

8.1 Budgeting for Small Businesses

A well-planned budget is crucial for financial stability and growth. Without a budget, it's like trying to drive across the country without a map—you're bound to get lost. A budget helps you allocate resources efficiently, track your progress, and stay focused on your financial goals. According to Forbes, businesses with structured budgets are better prepared to manage debt, evaluate performance, and handle emergencies. A staggering number of businesses fail within their first few years due to poor financial planning. The lack of a solid budget often leads to overspending, insufficient cash reserves, and ultimately, business failure.

The downfall of my first significant venture, which led to bankruptcy, can be traced back to inadequate budgeting. I placed too much trust in my initial sales forecasts, neglecting to adjust them as circumstances evolved. Moreover, my financial planning focused solely on projecting profits, overlooking the crucial aspect of cash flow management. This oversight meant that despite being profitable on paper, the business couldn't fulfill its payroll obligations, culminating in its inevitable failure.

Creating a detailed budget involves several steps. Start by categorizing your expenses into fixed, variable, and discretionary. Fixed expenses are those that remain constant each month, such as rent, insurance, and salaries. Variable expenses fluctuate based on your business activity, like utilities and raw materials. Discretionary expenses are non-essential costs that can be adjusted based on your budget, such as marketing campaigns or office decor. Once you've categorized your expenses, estimate your revenue and project future income. Look at your past sales data and market trends to make informed estimates. This helps you set realistic financial goals and understand your cash flow needs.

Tools and software can simplify the budgeting process. QuickBooks is a popular choice for small businesses, offering features like income and expense tracking, budget creation tools, and customizable financial reports. Xero is another excellent option, known for its user-friendly interface and robust features. For those who prefer manual budgeting, templates and spreadsheets can be equally effective. The key is to find a system that works for you and stick to it. Consistency in tracking and updating your budget is vital for maintaining financial health.

Maintaining and adjusting your budget is an ongoing process. Regular reviews allow you to compare your actual performance against your projections and make necessary adjustments. Conduct monthly budget reviews to identify any discrepancies and address them promptly. If you notice that your variable expenses are consistently higher than expected, look for ways to cut costs or adjust your revenue projections. Setting aside an emergency fund is also crucial. This reserve can help you weather unexpected expenses without derailing your budget. Aim to save at least three to six months' worth of operating expenses in your emergency fund.

8.2 Checklist: Practical Budgeting Tips

- Categorize Expenses: Divide expenses into fixed, variable, and discretionary.
- Estimate Revenue: Use past sales data and market trends for informed projections.
- Use Budgeting Tools: QuickBooks, Xero, or manual templates and spreadsheets.
- Monthly Reviews: Regularly compare actual performance against projections.
- Adjust as Needed: Cut costs or adjust revenue projections based on performance.
- Emergency Fund: Save three to six months' worth of operating expenses.

A well-planned budget is your financial roadmap, guiding you through the ups and downs of running a business. It helps you allocate resources efficiently, track your progress, and stay focused on your financial goals. With the right tools and regular reviews, you can maintain a healthy budget and ensure your business's long-term success.

8.3 Managing Cash Flow

Understanding cash flow is like understanding the lifeblood of your business. Cash flow refers to the movement of money in and out of your business. It's different from profit, which is the amount of money left after all expenses have been deducted from revenue. While profit is important, cash flow is what keeps your business running day-to-day. In my initial venture, I encountered a perplexing situation that led me to question my accountant, "If we're making a profit, why are we struggling to pay the bills?" This moment marked my introduction to the critical distinction between profit and cash flow. You can be profitable on paper but still struggle to pay your bills if your cash flow is mismanaged. For instance, I once knew a small retail business that had impressive sales and strong profit margins. However, they struggled to stay afloat because their cash was tied up in inventory and they weren't collecting payments from customers quickly enough. This ultimately led to their downfall.

To improve cash flow, you need to take actionable steps. One effective strategy is to speed up your invoice collections. Ensure that your invoicing process is efficient, and don't hesitate to follow up on late payments. Offering small discounts for early payments can incentivize customers to pay sooner. Another strategy is to negotiate longer payment terms with your suppliers. This gives you more time to pay your bills and keeps more cash in your business for longer periods. Implementing a cash reserve policy is also crucial. Set aside a portion of your revenue each month to build a cash reserve. This reserve can act as a buffer during lean periods, ensuring you have funds available when you need them most.

Using the right tools and techniques can make cash flow management much easier. Cash flow management software like Float and Pulse can help you monitor and manage your cash flow effectively. These tools offer features like cash flow forecasting, which allows you to predict your future cash flow based on current data. This helps you plan ahead and make informed decisions. Regularly reviewing your cash flow forecasts enables you to identify potential shortfalls and take corrective action before they become major issues. These tools can also help you track your receivables and payables, giving you a clear picture of where your money is going and when it's coming in.

Handling cash flow crises requires a calm and strategic approach. One option is to secure short-term financing, such as a line of credit or a short-term loan. This can provide you with the immediate funds needed to cover expenses. However, it's important to use these options wisely and ensure you can repay them in a timely manner. Cutting non-essential expenses temporarily can also help. Review your budget and identify areas where you can reduce costs without impacting your core operations. This might include delaying non-urgent purchases or renegotiating service contracts. Communicating with stakeholders about your cash flow challenges is also vital. Whether it's suppliers, employees, or investors, keeping them informed and involved can lead to collaborative solutions. For example, a supplier might be willing to extend your payment terms if they understand your situation.

In my second business, I faced a significant cash flow crisis. We had a large order from a major client, but they delayed payment, leaving us struggling to cover our expenses. I quickly realized the importance of having a cash reserve and a plan for such situations. By negotiating extended payment terms with our suppliers and cutting back on non-essential expenses, we managed to navigate through the crisis. It was a stressful time, but it taught me invaluable lessons about the importance of cash flow management.

Effective cash flow management is vital for the survival and growth of your business. By speeding up invoice collections, negotiating longer payment terms, and using cash flow management tools, you can maintain a positive cash flow. Additionally, having strategies in place for handling cash flow crises ensures you're prepared for any financial challenges that come your way. Whether you're just starting out or looking to improve your existing business, focusing on cash flow can make all the difference.

8.4 Understanding Financial Statements

Navigating the world of financial statements can seem daunting, but these documents are vital for understanding your business's financial health. Let's start with the three key financial statements: the Income Statement, the Balance Sheet, and the Cash Flow Statement. Each serves a unique purpose in providing insight into different aspects of your business.

The Income Statement, also known as the Profit and Loss Statement, summarizes your revenue, expenses, and profits over a specific period. This statement tells you how much money your business made and spent, and whether you ended up with a profit or a loss. Key components include revenue, cost of goods sold (COGS), gross profit, operating expenses, and net income. For instance, if your revenue for the month is $50,000, and your COGS is $20,000, your gross profit is $30,000. Subtract operating expenses like rent, salaries, and utilities, and you get your net income.

The Balance Sheet provides a snapshot of your business's financial position at a specific point in time. It lists your assets, liabilities, and equity. Think of it as a summary of what you own and owe. Assets include cash, inventory, and equipment. Liabilities are things like loans and accounts payable. Equity represents the owner's stake in the business. The fundamental equation here is Assets = Liabilities + Equity. If you have $100,000 in assets, $60,000 in liabilities, and $40,000 in equity, your balance sheet is balanced.

The Cash Flow Statement details the cash inflows and outflows during a specific period. It's divided into three sections: operating activities, investing activities, and financing activities. Operating activities include day-to-day transactions like sales and expenses. Investing activities cover the purchase and sale of long-term assets, such as equipment. Financing activities involve transactions related to debt and equity, like taking out loans or issuing shares. This statement is crucial for assessing your business's ability to generate cash and sustain operations. Unlike the Income Statement, which can include non-cash items like depreciation, the Cash Flow Statement focuses solely on actual cash movements.

Reading and interpreting these financial statements involves more than just glancing at the numbers. Start with the Income Statement to understand your profitability. Look at your revenue trends and compare them with your expenses. Calculate your gross profit margin (gross profit divided by revenue) to see how efficiently you're producing your goods or services. Next, examine the Balance Sheet to assess your financial stability. Calculate the current ratio (current assets divided by current liabilities) to gauge your ability to pay short-term obligations. A ratio above 1 indicates good short-term financial health. Also, consider the debt-to-equity ratio (total liabilities divided by total equity) to understand your leverage. A higher ratio means more debt, which can be risky.

Regular financial reviews are essential for making informed business decisions. Conduct monthly, quarterly, and annual reviews to stay on top of your financial health. Monthly reviews help you catch issues early and make timely adjustments. Quarterly reviews provide a broader perspective, allowing you to spot trends and make strategic decisions. Annual reviews give you a comprehensive view of your financial performance over the year, helping you plan for the future. Adjust your business strategies based on these insights. For example, if you notice that your operating expenses are consistently high, you might explore cost-cutting measures or renegotiate supplier contracts.

Working with financial professionals can provide valuable expertise and guidance. When selecting a qualified accountant or financial advisor, look for credentials like CPA (Certified Public Accountant) or CFA (Chartered Financial Analyst). Ask about their experience with businesses similar to yours. During financial reviews, prepare a list of questions to maximize the value of your consultations. Inquire about your financial statements, ask for advice on improving profitability, and discuss tax planning strategies. Regular consultations with financial professionals can help you navigate complex financial issues, ensure compliance with regulations, and optimize your financial health.

8.5 Strategies for Cost Reduction

Cost management is not just about keeping expenses low; it's about making sure every dollar spent contributes to the business's growth and sustainability. Controlling costs is crucial for profitability and ensuring your business can weather financial challenges. Take, for example, a small tech startup I once knew. By meticulously managing their costs, they were able to survive the critical early stages and eventually grow into a thriving company. On the flip side, numerous businesses fail due to poor cost management, often overspending on non-essential items while neglecting areas that could drive growth.

Reducing fixed and variable costs can significantly improve your business's financial health. Start by negotiating better terms with your suppliers. This doesn't mean just asking for discounts—consider longer-term contracts or bulk purchasing to get better rates. I recall negotiating a long-term contract with a key supplier, which saved us a considerable amount each year. Outsourcing non-core activities is another effective strategy. Tasks like payroll, customer service, or IT support can be outsourced to specialized firms, freeing up your resources to focus on your core business activities. Additionally, implementing energy-saving measures can lower your utility bills. Simple actions like switching to LED lighting, optimizing heating and cooling systems, and encouraging energy-saving habits among employees can make a big difference.

Technology plays a significant role in cost reduction. Automation tools can handle repetitive tasks such as data entry, invoicing, and email marketing, freeing up your team to focus on more strategic activities. For instance, using tools like Zapier to automate workflows can save countless hours. Cloud-based solutions can also reduce IT expenses. Instead of investing in expensive servers and IT infrastructure, opt for cloud services that offer scalable storage and computing power. This not only cuts costs but also provides flexibility to scale as your business grows. Collaboration tools like Slack or Microsoft Teams can minimize travel and office expenses by facilitating remote work and virtual meetings. These tools enable efficient communication and collaboration without the need for physical presence, further reducing costs.

Maintaining a lean operation offers numerous benefits, including increased efficiency, reduced waste, and improved profitability. Adopting lean manufacturing principles can streamline your production processes, ensuring that resources are used optimally and waste is minimized. For example, implementing techniques like 5S (Sort, Set in order, Shine, Standardize, Sustain) can organize your workspace and improve efficiency. Just-in-time inventory management is another powerful strategy. By ordering inventory only as needed, you can reduce storage costs and minimize the risk of overstocking. Regularly reviewing and optimizing processes is also crucial. Conduct periodic audits of your operations to identify inefficiencies and areas for improvement. This proactive approach ensures that your business remains agile and can quickly adapt to changes.

In my early days, I learned the hard way that ignoring cost management can lead to serious financial troubles. I once spent a significant amount on a fancy office space, thinking it would impress clients. It didn't. Instead, it drained our finances and added unnecessary stress. That experience taught me the importance of prioritizing expenses that directly contribute to business growth. By focusing on cost-effective strategies and leveraging technology, we were able to streamline operations and improve profitability.

Cost management is a continuous process that requires vigilance and adaptability. By negotiating better terms with suppliers, outsourcing non-core activities, and implementing energy-saving measures, you can reduce both fixed and variable costs. Leveraging technology through automation, cloud-based solutions, and collaboration tools can further streamline operations and cut expenses.

Maintaining a lean operation through lean manufacturing principles, just-in-time inventory management, and regular process reviews ensures that your business remains efficient and profitable.

Managing finances effectively is crucial for the success and sustainability of your business. By focusing on budgeting, cash flow management, understanding financial statements, and cost reduction, you can build a strong financial foundation. This foundation not only supports day-to-day operations but also prepares you for future growth and challenges. As we move forward, let's explore strategies for scaling your business and ensuring long-term success.

Chapter 9
Scaling Your Business

Let's delve into the strategies essential for transforming your business into a more substantial entity:

- Uncovering Opportunities for Scalability
- Activity: Pinpointing Your Unique Strengths
- Assembling and Nurturing Your Team
- Broadening Your Customer Base
- Utilizing Technological Advances for Expansion
- Action Plan: Keeping Abreast of Technological Developments

When I first realized the potential of my business, the thought of scaling it seemed both exciting and daunting. Scaling isn't just about growing bigger; it's about growing smarter. It's about expanding your reach without burning out or losing the quality that made your business special in the first place. For those aspiring to break free from the limitations of their current employment—be it early retirees seeking a new venture, empty-nesters aiming to fill their newfound time, or young individuals keen on carving their own paths—the concept of scalability is fundamental.

9.1 Identifying Scalable Opportunities

Scalability is the capacity of your business to grow and manage increased demand without compromising performance. It's the difference between a business that can grow exponentially and one that gets bogged down by its own success. Think about a software company that can sell millions of copies of its product without the need for additional physical infrastructure. That's a scalable model. In contrast, a custom furniture maker who handcrafts each piece may face challenges scaling due to the time-intensive nature of the work.

A scalable business typically has high margins and low incremental costs. High margins mean that the profit per unit is significant, while low incremental costs imply that scaling up production or services doesn't proportionately increase costs. For example, digital products like eBooks or online courses are highly scalable because, once created, they can be sold repeatedly with minimal additional costs. On the other hand, businesses heavily reliant on manual labor and physical resources often struggle to scale efficiently.

To identify scalable opportunities within your business, start by conducting a scalability audit. This involves evaluating your current operations to pinpoint areas with growth potential. Analyze your market trends and customer demands. Is there a growing need for a particular product or service you offer? Are there underserved markets that you could tap into? Evaluating your product or service offerings for scalability is also crucial. Consider whether your current offerings can be easily scaled or if they require significant customization and manual input.

Focusing on core competencies is essential when scaling your business. Core competencies are the unique strengths and abilities that set your business apart from the competition. These could be in the form of superior product quality, exceptional customer service, or innovative technology. By concentrating on these strengths, you can build a competitive advantage that is hard for others to replicate. For instance, Apple's focus on innovative design and user experience has been a core competency that drives its success. Outsourcing non-core activities, such as administrative tasks or IT support, can free up resources to focus on what you do best.

9.2 Exercise: Identifying Core Competencies

Take a moment to reflect on what makes your business unique. What do your customers value most about your products or services? What are the key strengths that differentiate you from competitors? Write these down and consider how you can leverage them to scale your business.

Case studies provide valuable insights into the importance of focusing on core competencies. Consider 3M, a company renowned for its innovation. By continuously developing new products and services, 3M has maintained a competitive edge and achieved significant growth. Another example is McDonald's, which focuses on providing consistent quality at a lower cost. This strategy has allowed McDonald's to scale globally while maintaining profitability.

Testing and validating scalable opportunities is a critical step before fully committing to them. Start by running small-scale pilot programs. These allow you to test new products or services with a limited audience, minimizing risk. Gather and analyze feedback from early adopters to identify any issues or areas for improvement. This feedback is invaluable in refining your offerings and ensuring they meet customer expectations. Adjust your strategies based on the pilot results. If the feedback is positive and the pilot demonstrates scalability, you can proceed with a larger rollout.

The journey to scaling your business is filled with both challenges and opportunities. By understanding the concept of scalability, identifying areas with growth potential, focusing on core competencies, and testing new initiatives, you can set your business on a path to sustainable growth. The key is to grow smarter, leveraging your strengths and continuously adapting to meet market demands. Scaling isn't just about getting bigger; it's about creating a business that can thrive in the long run.

9.3 Hiring and Building a Team

Building a strong team is crucial when scaling your business. A capable team supports growth by bringing diverse skills, perspectives, and energy to the table. When I first started expanding my business, I realized that having the right people by my side made all the difference. A case study of Google showcases this well. Google's initial team was small, but each member brought unique expertise, from coding to business strategy. This diversity in skills helped them scale rapidly. A study by McKinsey found that companies with diverse executive teams are 33% more likely to outperform their peers in profitability. Quality teams drive innovation, efficiency, and ultimately, success.

Attracting and hiring top talent is a strategic process. It starts with crafting compelling job descriptions. These should be clear, engaging, and aligned with your company's vision and values. Highlight what makes your company unique and why someone would want to work there. Use multiple recruitment channels to reach a broader audience. Job boards like Indeed and LinkedIn are effective, but don't overlook social media and employee referral programs. Social media can showcase your company culture, while employee referrals bring in candidates who fit well with the team dynamics. Conduct thorough interviews and assessments to ensure that candidates not only have the necessary skills but also align with your company's values. This can include technical tests, behavioral interviews, and culture-fit assessments.

Company culture plays a significant role in team building. A positive and productive work environment encourages employees to give their best. Defining and communicating your company values is the first step. These values should be more than just words on a wall; they should be lived and breathed daily by everyone in the company. Implement team-building activities and events to foster camaraderie. Whether it's a monthly team lunch, an annual retreat, or regular team-building exercises, these activities help build strong relationships and a sense of belonging. Encouraging open communication and feedback is also vital. Create an environment where employees feel comfortable sharing their ideas and concerns. Regular feedback sessions and open-door policies can help maintain this culture.

Developing and retaining employees is just as important as hiring them. Implement training and professional development programs to help your team grow. This can include workshops, online courses, or even mentorship programs. Offering competitive compensation and benefits is essential. While salary is important, benefits like health insurance, retirement plans, and paid time off can make a big difference. Think about offering flexible work arrangements, especially in today's remote work environment. Creating clear career advancement paths is another key factor in retention. Employees need to see a future with your company. Outline potential career paths and offer regular performance reviews to discuss their progress and goals.

Consider the example of HubSpot, which has been recognized for its exceptional company culture. HubSpot offers extensive training programs, clear career paths, and a supportive work environment. This has helped them attract and retain top talent, contributing to their rapid growth. They've also implemented innovative benefits like unlimited vacation days and remote work options, which have made them an employer of choice in the tech industry.

Incorporating these strategies into your hiring and team-building practices can set your business on the path to successful scaling. A strong team not only supports growth but also drives innovation and maintains the quality of your products or services. By focusing on building a positive company culture, attracting top talent, and investing in employee development, you create a foundation for sustainable growth and long-term success.

9.4 Expanding Your Market Reach

When I began expanding my own business, I quickly learned that market expansion is crucial for scaling. It's not just about growing bigger; it's about diversifying and finding new customer bases to ensure long-term success. Entering new markets can drive significant business growth by tapping into unserved or underserved customer bases. For instance, when Netflix expanded from DVD rentals to streaming and then into international markets, its growth skyrocketed. This shift not only increased their customer base but also diversified their revenue streams, making the company more resilient.

Identifying new market opportunities starts with thorough research. Begin by conducting comprehensive market research and analysis. This involves understanding the market size, competition, and demand in potential new markets. For example, if you're a tech startup considering expanding into Europe, study the tech adoption rates, existing competitors, and the specific needs of European consumers. Assess the market size to determine if it's large enough to support your business. Understanding the competition will help you identify gaps that your product or service can fill. Additionally, consider the demand for your offerings. Are potential customers in this new market actively seeking solutions like yours?

Identifying potential barriers to entry is another critical step. These barriers can include regulatory requirements, cultural differences, or logistical challenges. For instance, if you're a food business looking to expand internationally, you might face strict food safety regulations in different countries. Understanding these barriers ahead of time allows you to develop strategies to overcome them. This might involve partnering with local experts who understand the regulatory landscape or adapting your product to meet local tastes and preferences.

Once you've identified a new market, the next step is to establish a presence there. One effective method is partnering with local businesses or distributors. This approach allows you to leverage their existing infrastructure and customer base. For example, if you're a fashion brand entering a new country, partnering with local boutiques can help you reach customers more quickly. Tailoring your marketing and sales strategies to the new market segment is also crucial. What works in your home market might not resonate with customers in a new region. Adapt your messaging, promotions, and even your product offerings to align with local preferences.

Setting up local offices or distribution centers can further solidify your presence. This not only makes it easier to serve your new customers but also demonstrates your commitment to the market. Consider Amazon's strategy when expanding into India. They set up numerous fulfillment centers across the country to ensure fast and reliable delivery, catering to the specific needs of the Indian market. This investment paid off, as Amazon quickly became one of the leading e-commerce platforms in India.

Managing and sustaining market expansion requires continuous effort. Start by monitoring market performance and customer feedback closely. Use analytics tools to track key metrics like sales, customer acquisition costs, and customer satisfaction. This data helps you understand what's working and what needs adjustment. Listening to customer feedback is equally important. It provides insights into how your products or services are being received and what improvements can be made. Regularly soliciting feedback through surveys or social media can help you stay attuned to customer needs.

Adapting your products or services based on local preferences and needs is another key strategy. For instance, when Starbucks entered the Chinese market, they adapted their menu to include more tea-based beverages and local flavors. This approach helped them resonate with Chinese consumers and build a loyal customer base. Building strong relationships with local stakeholders, such as suppliers, community leaders, and industry influencers, can also support sustained growth. These relationships can provide valuable insights, resources, and support as you navigate the complexities of the new market.

Expanding your market reach is a multifaceted process that requires careful planning, adaptation, and continuous monitoring. By conducting thorough research, tailoring your strategies, and maintaining strong local relationships, you can successfully enter new markets and drive significant business growth.

9.5 Leveraging Technology for Growth

Technology plays a pivotal role in scaling a business. It supports and drives growth by streamlining operations, increasing efficiency, and enabling you to reach a broader audience. Take Uber, for example. They scaled rapidly by leveraging mobile technology to connect drivers and riders seamlessly. Similarly, Amazon's sophisticated logistics and inventory management systems have allowed them to dominate the e-commerce space. According to a study by McKinsey, businesses that adopt advanced digital technologies can increase productivity by up to 30%. This shows how crucial technology is for achieving scalability and efficiency.

Selecting the right technology solutions begins with a needs assessment. Start by identifying the areas where technology can have the most significant impact. Are you looking to improve customer relationship management, streamline operations, or enhance marketing efforts? Once you've pinpointed these areas, evaluate technology solutions based on scalability and return on investment (ROI). Look for tools that can grow with your business and offer a strong ROI. For example, investing in a robust Customer Relationship Management (CRM) system like Salesforce can help you manage customer interactions more effectively, leading to increased sales and customer retention. Implementing and integrating new technologies with your existing systems is the next step. This might involve training your team, migrating data, and ensuring that different systems can communicate with each other seamlessly.

Automation and artificial intelligence (AI) are game-changers when it comes to scaling a business. Automation can handle repetitive tasks, freeing up your team to focus on more strategic activities. For instance, tools like Zapier can automate workflows by connecting different apps and automating tasks such as data entry and email marketing. AI, on the other hand, can provide valuable insights and improve decision-making. Consider chatbots powered by AI that can handle customer inquiries 24/7, improving customer service without increasing staffing costs. Another example is AI-driven analytics tools that can analyze large datasets to identify trends and make predictions, helping you make data-driven decisions. A case study of a mid-sized retail company illustrates this well. By implementing AI-driven inventory management, they reduced stockouts by 20% and cut excess inventory by 15%, leading to significant cost savings and improved customer satisfaction.

Staying updated with technological advancements is crucial for maintaining a competitive edge. Participate in industry conferences and tech expos to learn about the latest trends and innovations. These events offer a wealth of knowledge and networking opportunities. Subscribing to tech-focused publications and blogs can also keep you informed about emerging technologies and best practices. Websites like TechCrunch and Wired provide regular updates on tech developments that could impact your business. Networking with other tech-savvy entrepreneurs and professionals is another valuable strategy. Join online forums, attend meetups, and engage with industry groups on social media platforms like LinkedIn. These interactions can provide insights, inspiration, and even potential collaborations.

9.6 Checklist: Staying Updated with Technology

1) Participate in Industry Conferences and Tech Expos: Gain firsthand knowledge of the latest trends and innovations.
2) Subscribe to Tech-Focused Publications and Blogs: Stay informed about emerging technologies and best practices.
3) Network with Tech-Savvy Entrepreneurs: Engage with online forums, attend meetups, and connect on LinkedIn.

By leveraging technology effectively, you can drive significant business growth. Whether it's through automation, AI, or staying updated with the latest tech trends, technology can provide the tools and insights needed to scale your business efficiently. As you integrate these strategies, you'll find that technology not only supports growth but also opens up new opportunities for innovation and improvement.

Chapter 10

Building a Strong Company Culture

The culture of a company is a pivotal factor that can significantly influence its growth trajectory. To harness the power of a positive company culture for the prosperity of your business, consider the following strategies:

- Establishing Your Company's Core Principles
- Discovering and Expressing Fundamental Values
- Embedding These Values into Everyday Business Practices
- Effective Methods for Communicating and Strengthening Values
- Cultivating a High Level of Employee Involvement
- Developing an Environment that Encourages Teamwork
- Advancing Continuous Education and Skill Development

When I first started my own business, I quickly realized that having a great product or service was only part of the equation. What really made a difference was the culture we built. And at the heart of that culture were our company values. These values acted as a compass, guiding our decisions and shaping the way we interacted with each other and our customers. If you're looking to break free from the constraints of your current job and create something truly meaningful, defining and living by your company values is crucial.

10.1 Defining Your Company Values

Company values are the foundation of any successful business. They provide a clear sense of purpose and direction, helping you make decisions that align with your long-term goals. Companies with strong value-driven cultures tend to thrive. Take Patagonia, for example. Their commitment to environmental sustainability isn't just a marketing gimmick; it's a core value that shapes every aspect of their business. This commitment has earned them a loyal customer base and a reputation for integrity. Similarly, Zappos' focus on exceptional customer service has created a culture where employees are empowered to go above and beyond for customers. This has not only boosted customer satisfaction but also employee morale and retention.

Statistics back this up. Organizations with clearly defined values see higher employee satisfaction and performance. According to a study by the Harvard Business Review, companies with strong cultures based on shared values experience a 72% higher employee engagement rate. This engagement translates to lower turnover rates, higher productivity, and ultimately, better financial performance. Clearly, defining and communicating your values can have a profound impact on your business's success.

10.2 Identifying and Articulating Core Values

So, how do you go about defining these all-important values? Start by conducting workshops with your leadership team and employees. These sessions should be collaborative, allowing everyone to contribute their thoughts and ideas. Reflect on your company's mission and vision. What are the principles that will guide you toward achieving your goals? Aligning your values with your long-term business objectives ensures they are not only aspirational but also practical.

Once you've brainstormed, distill these ideas into a list of core values. Aim for clarity and simplicity. Values like "integrity," "innovation," and "customer focus" are straightforward yet powerful. They should resonate with both your team and your customers. Make sure these values are not just words on a wall but principles that genuinely reflect the way you want to operate. For example, if one of your values is "transparency," ensure that you practice open communication at all levels of the organization.

10.3 Integrating Values into Daily Operations

Embedding your core values into every aspect of your business is essential for them to truly take root. Start with the hiring process. Look for candidates who not only have the skills you need but also share your values. During interviews, ask questions that reveal how they align with your company's principles. For instance, if "teamwork" is a core value, ask about their experiences working in teams and how they contributed to group success.

Onboarding is another critical phase for reinforcing values. New hires should be introduced to your company's values from day one. Include them in your onboarding materials and make sure they understand how these values shape your business practices. Use real-life examples and stories to illustrate how employees exemplify these values in their daily work. Performance evaluations should also reflect your core values. Assess employees not only on their job performance but also on how well they embody and promote your values. This reinforces their importance and encourages everyone to live by them.

Internal communication is a powerful tool for promoting and reinforcing your values. Share success stories that highlight employees who exemplify your values. Whether it's a newsletter feature or a shout-out in a team meeting, these stories keep your values top of mind and show that they are more than just words. Visual reminders can also be effective. Posters or digital displays in common areas can serve as constant reminders of what your company stands for.

Encouraging leaders to model these values is perhaps the most impactful way to embed them into your culture. Employees look to their leaders for cues on behavior and decision-making. When leaders consistently demonstrate the company's values through their actions, it sets a powerful example for the rest of the team. For instance, if "customer focus" is a core value, leaders should prioritize customer needs in their decisions and interactions. This creates a culture where values are lived and breathed daily.

10.4 Tips for Communicating and Reinforcing Values

Regularly sharing value-based success stories is one of the most effective ways to communicate and reinforce your values. These stories can be shared in team meetings, newsletters, or even social media platforms. They not only highlight the importance of your values but also recognize and celebrate employees who embody them. Creating visual reminders, such as posters or digital displays in the workplace, keeps your values visible and top-of-mind.

Encouraging leaders to model your values is crucial. Leaders set the tone for the entire organization, and their actions speak louder than words. When leaders consistently demonstrate your values, it sends a strong message to the rest of the team about what is important. For example, if "integrity" is one of your values, leaders should always act with honesty and transparency, even when it's difficult. This builds trust and reinforces the importance of your values.

Building a strong company culture rooted in clearly defined values is essential for guiding behavior and decision-making within your organization. By identifying and articulating your core values, integrating them into daily operations, and effectively communicating and reinforcing them, you can create a culture that supports your long-term business goals and enhances employee satisfaction and performance.

10.5 Fostering Employee Engagement

Engaged employees are your business's best asset. They bring higher productivity, better customer service, and lower turnover rates. Consider Google, where employee engagement is a cornerstone of their success. Google's innovative work environment—think nap pods, free meals, and open communication—keeps employees motivated and loyal. Similarly, Southwest Airlines involves employees in critical decisions, like designing new uniforms, which fosters a sense of ownership and pride. According to a Gallup study, companies with high employee engagement see 21% higher profitability and 17% higher productivity. These numbers aren't just impressive; they're a testament to the tangible benefits of keeping your team engaged.

Measuring engagement levels is your first step. Employee engagement surveys are a practical tool. These surveys can include questions about job satisfaction, alignment with company goals, and overall workplace happiness. Use tools like SurveyMonkey or Google Forms to create and distribute these surveys anonymously. Analyzing the results can give you a clear picture of your team's engagement level. Additionally, holding focus groups provides deeper insights. These small group discussions allow employees to voice their opinions and offer suggestions. One-on-one interviews can also be enlightening, revealing individual concerns and aspirations. Metrics like retention rates and absenteeism are also telling indicators. High retention and low absenteeism often signal a happy, engaged workforce.

Improving engagement involves creating a work environment that people want to be a part of. Start by offering meaningful work. Employees want to know that what they do matters. When assigning tasks, explain how their work contributes to the company's goals. Clear career paths are also crucial. No one wants to feel stuck in a dead-end job. Show employees how they can grow within the company. Recognizing and rewarding achievements can't be overstated. A simple thank-you note or a shout-out during a meeting can go a long way.

Consider implementing an employee recognition program where peers can nominate each other for awards. Open communication is another key factor. Encourage feedback and make it easy for employees to share their thoughts. Use tools like Slack or Microsoft Teams for real-time communication and feedback.

Providing opportunities for employee input in decision-making can also boost engagement. When employees feel that their opinions matter, they are more likely to be committed to their work. Involve them in brainstorming sessions and strategy meetings. This not only makes them feel valued but also brings diverse perspectives to the table. For example, when planning a new project, gather input from different departments. This cross-functional approach can lead to more innovative solutions and a more cohesive team.

Maintaining high levels of engagement requires ongoing effort. Regularly review and update your engagement strategies. What worked last year might not be as effective now. Hosting team-building activities and social events can also help maintain engagement. These activities don't have to be extravagant. Simple events like a monthly team lunch or a casual Friday game session can strengthen team bonds. Ensuring work-life balance is equally important. Encourage employees to take breaks and use their vacation days. Implement well-being initiatives like flexible work hours, wellness programs, and mental health support. When employees feel that their well-being is a priority, they are more likely to stay engaged.

Roy Nabors at Southwest Airlines is a great example of how engagement can transform an employee's experience. Involved in designing new uniforms, Roy felt a deep connection to the company. This sense of belonging and contribution turned into higher motivation and job satisfaction. Engaged employees are not just happier; they are more productive, loyal, and innovative. Creating an environment where employees feel valued and heard is not just good for them; it's good for your business. Regularly assess engagement levels, offer meaningful work, recognize achievements, and maintain a healthy work-life balance. These steps can help you build a team that's not just present but fully engaged in helping your business succeed.

10.6 Creating a Collaborative Work Environment

Collaboration within a work environment can be a game-changer. It fosters innovation, enhances problem-solving, and significantly boosts employee satisfaction. When employees work together, they bring diverse perspectives that can lead to groundbreaking ideas. Pixar is a shining example of this. Their open workspaces and culture of candid feedback have led to a string of successful films. At IDEO, collaboration is woven into the fabric of their operations. Teams from different disciplines come together to brainstorm and prototype, resulting in innovative solutions for clients. According to a study by the Institute for Corporate Productivity, companies that promote collaborative working are five times more likely to be high-performing. These statistics underscore the tangible benefits of fostering a collaborative culture.

Creating a collaborative environment starts with the physical workspace. Open and flexible workspaces encourage spontaneous interactions and make it easier for teams to work together. Consider incorporating communal areas where employees can gather for informal meetings. Collaborative tools and platforms like Slack and Microsoft Teams are also invaluable. These tools facilitate communication and collaboration, allowing team members to share ideas and work on projects in real-time, regardless of their physical location. Cross-functional projects and teams further enhance collaboration. When people from different departments come together to tackle a project, they bring unique skills and perspectives that can lead to more innovative solutions. For instance, a marketing team working with a product development team can create campaigns that are not only creative but also technically feasible.

Leadership plays a crucial role in promoting collaboration. Leaders must model collaborative behavior by working closely with their teams and encouraging open communication. Facilitating team-building exercises and workshops can help strengthen bonds among team members and improve their ability to work together. These activities don't have to be elaborate. Simple exercises like problem-solving games or collaborative brainstorming sessions can be very effective. Providing training on effective collaboration and communication skills is also essential. This can include workshops on active listening, conflict resolution, and constructive feedback. When employees are equipped with these skills, they are more likely to collaborate effectively.

However, fostering collaboration is not without its challenges. One common barrier is conflict. Addressing and resolving conflicts promptly is crucial to maintaining a collaborative environment. Encourage open dialogue and create a safe space where employees feel comfortable expressing their concerns. Breaking down silos is another challenge. Silos occur when departments or teams work in isolation, hindering collaboration. Encourage information sharing and cross-departmental communication to break down these barriers. Regular meetings where different departments update each other on their projects can be very effective. Ensuring diversity and inclusion in team compositions is also vital. Diverse teams bring a variety of perspectives and ideas, leading to more innovative solutions. Make sure to include individuals with different backgrounds, skills, and experiences in your teams.

In a collaborative environment, everyone feels valued and heard. People are more willing to share their ideas and work together towards common goals. This not only leads to better business outcomes but also creates a positive work culture where employees are engaged and motivated. Creating a collaborative work environment is about more than just open spaces and tools. It requires a commitment from leadership to model and promote collaborative behavior, as well as a willingness to address challenges head-on. By fostering a culture of collaboration, you can unlock the full potential of your team and drive your business towards greater success.

10.7 Implementing Continuous Learning Programs

Continuous learning is more than just a buzzword; it's a vital part of any thriving business. When employees are encouraged to continuously improve their skills, they not only grow professionally but also contribute more effectively to the company's success. IBM and AT&T are prime examples of companies that prioritize continuous learning. IBM's extensive online learning platform offers courses from coding to leadership, helping employees stay current in a rapidly changing tech landscape. AT&T invests heavily in reskilling programs, ensuring their workforce is always equipped with the latest skills. According to a LinkedIn report, companies that invest in continuous learning see a 94% higher employee retention rate. Moreover, businesses that provide learning opportunities are 92% more likely to innovate and 37% more productive.

Creating a culture of continuous learning starts with a solid learning and development plan aligned with your business goals. This plan should identify the skills needed for future growth and outline the steps to acquire them. Offering a variety of learning opportunities keeps employees engaged and motivated. Workshops, online courses, and mentoring programs cater to different learning styles and preferences. Encourage a growth mindset by promoting curiosity and the idea that skills can always be developed. This mindset helps employees embrace challenges and view failures as learning opportunities.

Delivering effective training programs is crucial for fostering continuous learning. E-learning platforms like Coursera and LinkedIn Learning provide a vast array of courses that employees can take at their own pace. These platforms offer certifications and badges that can be shared on professional networks, adding an element of recognition and achievement. Hosting in-house training sessions and workshops brings learning into the workplace, making it more accessible. Partnering with external experts and instructors can also provide fresh perspectives and specialized knowledge. For example, bringing in a cybersecurity expert to train your IT team can provide insights that go beyond basic online courses.

Assessing the impact of your learning programs ensures they are effective and aligned with your goals. Collect feedback from participants through surveys and one-on-one discussions. This feedback can highlight areas for improvement and provide insights into what employees find most valuable. Tracking key performance indicators (KPIs) related to learning outcomes, such as course completion rates, skill acquisition, and application of new skills in the workplace, helps measure the success of your programs. Adjust your learning initiatives based on this data to ensure they remain relevant and effective.

Conclusion

Implementing continuous learning programs is an investment in your employees and your business's future. It fosters a culture of growth, innovation, and adaptability, ensuring that your team is always equipped with the skills needed to succeed. By creating a learning and development plan, offering diverse learning opportunities, delivering effective training, and assessing the impact of your programs, you can build a workforce that is engaged, skilled, and ready to take on new challenges. As we move forward, let's explore how maintaining business agility can further enhance your company's resilience and success.

Chapter 11
Navigating Challenges

Navigating the hurdles of entrepreneurship entails addressing inevitable challenges without becoming overwhelmed. This journey includes:

- Strategies for Stress Management and Burnout Prevention
- A Reflective Exercise on Pinpointing Stress Inducers
- Techniques for Adapting to Market Evolutions
- Insights from Netflix's Evolution from DVDs to Streaming
- Approaches to Overcome Business Obstacles
- Principles for Sustaining a Healthy Work-Life Equilibrium

Starting your own business is both thrilling and daunting. One moment you're riding high on the excitement of a new venture, and the next, you're bogged down by stress and burnout. When I first ventured into entrepreneurship, I didn't anticipate the toll it would take on my mental and physical health. The high workload, the pressure to meet financial targets, and the constant hustle left me feeling drained and overwhelmed. If you're seeking independence from your current job or starting a second career, understanding and managing stress is crucial. Let's delve into the common causes and symptoms of stress and burnout and explore practical strategies to manage them.

11.1 Managing Stress and Avoiding Burnout

Stress in entrepreneurship often stems from juggling multiple roles, working long hours, and the relentless pressure to hit financial milestones. You might find yourself working late into the night, sacrificing weekends, and constantly worrying about cash flow. Over time, this relentless pace can lead to chronic fatigue, insomnia, and decreased productivity. You might notice that tasks that once seemed manageable now feel overwhelming, and your enthusiasm starts to wane. It's essential to recognize these signs early and take proactive steps to manage stress before it spirals into burnout.

One effective way to manage stress is through mindfulness and meditation. Practicing mindfulness helps you stay present and focused, reducing the mind's tendency to ruminate over past mistakes or future worries. Mindfulness meditation involves simple techniques like focusing on your breath, observing your thoughts without judgment, and practicing deep breathing exercises. Studies show that regular mindfulness practice can lower stress levels and improve overall well-being (Source: Mindful). Engaging in regular physical exercise is another powerful stress buster. Whether it's a morning jog, yoga, or even a brisk walk, physical activity releases endorphins that boost your mood and energy levels.

Setting boundaries is also crucial in managing stress. As an entrepreneur, it's easy to fall into the trap of saying yes to every opportunity or request, fearing that turning something down might mean missing out. However, learning to say no when necessary protects your time and energy. Establishing clear work hours and sticking to them can help maintain a healthy work-life balance. Communicate your boundaries to family, friends, and colleagues to ensure they understand and respect your need for personal time.

Self-care and mental health should be top priorities. Scheduling regular breaks and vacations is not just a luxury but a necessity to recharge and prevent burnout. Taking time off allows you to return to your business with renewed energy and fresh perspectives. Seeking professional support, such as therapy or counseling, can provide valuable tools and coping strategies. Engaging in hobbies and activities that bring joy and relaxation is equally important. Whether it's reading, gardening, or painting, make time for activities that nourish your soul.

Creating a supportive work environment is another key factor in reducing stress. Encourage open communication about stress and mental health within your team. Let your employees know that it's okay to speak up if they're feeling overwhelmed. Implementing flexible work schedules can help accommodate different working styles and personal commitments. Providing access to wellness programs and resources, such as gym memberships or mindfulness workshops, shows that you value your team's well-being.

11.2 Reflection Section: Identifying Your Stress Triggers

Take a moment to reflect on your own experiences with stress and burnout. What are the specific triggers that cause you the most stress? Is it the long hours, the financial pressure, or the constant juggling of tasks? Write down your thoughts and consider how you can address these triggers. For example, if financial pressure is a significant stressor, you might focus on improving your budgeting and cash flow management. If long hours are wearing you down, look at ways to delegate tasks or streamline operations. Identifying your stress triggers is the first step in managing them effectively.

In the end, managing stress and avoiding burnout is about finding balance. It's about recognizing when you need to step back and recharge, and understanding that taking care of yourself is not a sign of weakness but a necessary part of running a successful business. By incorporating mindfulness, setting boundaries, prioritizing self-care, and fostering a supportive work environment, you can navigate the challenges of entrepreneurship with resilience and grace.

11.3 Adapting to Market Changes

In the world of business, adaptability is not just a nice-to-have trait; it's a necessity for long-term success. Companies that can't pivot when the market shifts often find themselves left behind. Take Netflix, for example. Initially a mail-order DVD rental service, Netflix saw the writing on the wall as digital streaming became more viable. They pivoted, investing heavily in streaming technology and original content. The result? Netflix became a global giant, fundamentally changing how we consume media (Source: Netflix Case Study). Similarly, Amazon started as an online bookstore but quickly expanded into various sectors, from cloud computing to groceries. Their ability to adapt has made them one of the most valuable companies in the world.

Staying informed about market trends is crucial. One of the simplest ways to keep your finger on the pulse is by subscribing to industry publications and newsletters. These sources offer insights into emerging trends, technological advancements, and shifting consumer behaviors. Attending trade shows, conferences, and webinars can also provide valuable learning opportunities. Here, you can network with industry peers, attend panel discussions, and get a firsthand look at new products and innovations. Networking with thought leaders and other entrepreneurs is another effective way to stay updated. Engaging in conversations, whether online or in person, can offer perspectives you might not find in articles or reports.

Once you're informed, the next step is to evaluate and respond to these market changes. Regular SWOT analyses (assessing strengths, weaknesses, opportunities, and threats) can help you stay proactive. For instance, if a new competitor enters the market, a SWOT analysis can help you identify your unique strengths and how to leverage them. Customer feedback is another invaluable resource. By listening to your customers, you can identify pain points and areas for improvement. This feedback can inform strategic adjustments, whether it's tweaking your product offerings or revising your marketing strategy. Sometimes, responding to market shifts requires a more significant pivot. This could mean altering your business model or launching a new product line. The key is to remain flexible and willing to make changes when necessary.

Fostering a culture of innovation within your organization is essential for adaptability. Encourage creativity and continuous improvement by implementing brainstorming sessions and ideation workshops. These activities can generate fresh ideas and solutions to existing problems. Setting up cross-functional teams can also drive innovation. When people from different departments collaborate, they bring diverse perspectives and expertise to the table, often leading to more innovative solutions. Rewarding and recognizing innovative ideas can further encourage a culture of creativity. Whether it's through bonuses, public recognition, or career advancement opportunities, showing appreciation for innovative efforts can motivate your team to keep pushing boundaries.

11.4 Case Study: Netflix's Digital Transformation

Netflix's shift from a DVD rental service to a streaming giant is a prime example of adaptability. Initially, Netflix offered a convenient alternative to traditional video rental stores by mailing DVDs directly to customers. However, as internet speeds improved and streaming technology became more viable, the company saw an opportunity. In 2007, Netflix introduced streaming alongside its DVD rental service. This move allowed them to stay ahead of the curve as consumer preferences shifted towards digital content. By 2019, Netflix had allocated $15 billion for new content creation, further solidifying its position in the market. Today, Netflix's valuation has soared, thanks in large part to its ability to adapt and innovate (Source: Netflix Case Study).

To thrive in an ever-changing market, businesses must be proactive, informed, and flexible. Adaptability involves not only staying current with industry trends but also being willing to make strategic adjustments based on those insights. By fostering a culture of innovation and continuously seeking ways to improve, you can ensure your business remains resilient and competitive in the face of change.

11.5 Handling Business Setbacks

Setbacks are an inevitable part of entrepreneurship. They don't mean you've failed; they're simply bumps in the road that every successful entrepreneur faces. Even the most iconic entrepreneurs have had their share of setbacks. Steve Jobs was famously ousted from Apple, the company he co-founded, only to return years later and lead it to unprecedented success. J.K. Rowling, before becoming a household name, faced numerous rejections for her Harry Potter manuscript. These stories remind us that setbacks are not the end but often the beginning of something greater.

Statistics show that about 20% of small businesses fail within their first year, and 50% fail within five years. Understanding this can help you see that encountering challenges is normal and not a reflection of your abilities. What matters is how you respond to these setbacks. Developing resilience and perseverance is key. Start by practicing positive self-talk. When negative thoughts creep in, counter them with affirmations. Instead of thinking, "I can't do this," say, "I'm capable of handling this challenge." Reframing your thoughts can significantly impact your mental toughness.

Setting realistic expectations is another important strategy. Don't aim for perfection; aim for progress. Celebrate small wins along the way. Did you secure a new client? That's a win. Did you improve your product? Another win. These small victories add up and keep you motivated. Building a strong support network is also crucial. Surround yourself with mentors, peers, and friends who can offer encouragement and advice. They can provide different perspectives and help you see solutions you might have missed.

When setbacks occur, take the time to analyze and learn from them. Conduct a post-mortem analysis to identify the root causes. Ask yourself what went wrong and why. Was it a lack of market research? Poor financial planning? Understanding the root cause helps you make informed changes. Implement these changes based on the lessons learned. If you discover that your marketing strategy was ineffective, try a new approach. Share your experiences with your team. This fosters collective growth and ensures that everyone learns from the setback, not just you.

Maintaining motivation during challenging times can be difficult, but it's not impossible. Set short-term, achievable goals to keep yourself focused and motivated. These goals act as stepping stones, making the bigger picture less overwhelming. Remind yourself of the long-term vision. Why did you start this business? What do you hope to achieve? Keeping the bigger picture in mind can help you push through tough times. Seek inspiration from success stories and motivational content. Read about other entrepreneurs who faced setbacks but persevered. Their stories can offer valuable lessons and keep you motivated.

One of the best ways to handle setbacks is to reframe them as learning opportunities. Instead of seeing them as failures, view them as experiences that bring you closer to your goals. Each setback teaches you something new, whether it's about your market, your product, or yourself. This mindset shift can make a significant difference in how you approach challenges. It helps you stay positive and focused on growth rather than getting bogged down by setbacks.

Remember, setbacks are not the end of the road. They're part of the entrepreneurial journey. Developing resilience and perseverance, learning from your mistakes, and staying motivated will help you navigate these challenges. Keep pushing forward, and don't let setbacks define your path. They're just detours on the way to success.

11.6 Maintaining Work-Life Balance

Balancing work and personal life is a cornerstone of a fulfilling entrepreneurial experience. Entrepreneurs like Richard Branson emphasize the importance of this balance. Branson, despite his numerous ventures, prioritizes family time and personal well-being. This balance has not only contributed to his happiness but also to his productivity and creativity. Studies show that maintaining a healthy work-life balance can boost productivity by up to 21% and significantly improve mental health. Without this balance, you risk burnout, decreased efficiency, and strained relationships.

Creating a clear separation between work and personal life is crucial. Start by setting specific work hours and sticking to them. Decide when your workday begins and ends, and make it a point to adhere to this schedule. This helps in creating a routine and ensures that work doesn't spill over into your personal time. Physical and mental boundaries are equally important. If possible, create a dedicated workspace that you leave when your work hours are over. This physical separation helps signal to your brain that work time is over and it's time to unwind. Communicate these boundaries to your family, friends, and colleagues. Let them know your work hours and ask for their support in respecting these boundaries. This communication helps manage expectations and reduces interruptions during work hours.

Prioritizing personal well-being is not just a luxury; it's a necessity. Make time for regular exercise and relaxation activities. Whether it's a morning jog, yoga, or a simple walk in the park, physical activity can rejuvenate your mind and body. Spend quality time with family and friends. These relationships provide emotional support, joy, and a sense of belonging that work cannot replace. Pursue hobbies and interests outside of work. Engaging in activities you love can be a great stress reliever and can bring a sense of accomplishment and satisfaction. Whether it's painting, gardening, or playing an instrument, make time for these activities.

Effective time management is key to achieving a healthy work-life balance. Using time management tools and techniques can help you stay organized and focused. Techniques like time-blocking, where you allocate specific blocks of time to different tasks, can help you manage your day more efficiently. The Pomodoro Technique, which involves working in short, focused intervals followed by short breaks, can improve productivity and prevent burnout. Delegate tasks whenever possible. You don't have to do everything yourself. Leverage your team's skills and delegate tasks that can be handled by others. This not only lightens your load but also empowers your team. Regularly review and adjust your priorities. Your business and personal needs will change over time. Periodic reviews can help you adjust your schedule and priorities to ensure you maintain a healthy balance.

Maintaining work-life balance is not a one-time task but an ongoing process. It requires constant attention and adjustments. By setting clear boundaries, prioritizing personal well-being, and managing your time effectively, you can create a balance that not only enhances your well-being but also contributes to your business success.

Incorporating these strategies can make a significant difference in your entrepreneurial journey. Balancing the demands of running a business with personal well-being is challenging but entirely possible. With the right approach, you can enjoy the best of both worlds, ensuring a fulfilling and successful entrepreneurial experience. Now, let's look ahead to the next chapter, where we'll explore ensuring long-term success in your business endeavors.

Chapter 12
Ensuring Long-Term Success

Now that you've established a thriving business, the next step is to ensure its longevity and continued success:

- Creating a Legacy with Your Business
- Reflecting on Your Legacy Vision
- Embracing a Mindset of Continuous Improvement
- A Guide to Promoting Continuous Improvement
- Securing Your Business for the Future
- A Checklist for Future-Proofing Your Business Maximizing Growth

When I started my first business, I was driven by more than just the desire to escape the corporate grind. I wanted to create something that would last, something that would make a difference long after I was gone. That's when I realized the importance of building a legacy. A legacy isn't just about short-term success or making a quick profit. It's about creating a lasting impact that resonates with your values, impacts your community positively, and stands the test of time. Think about companies like Walt Disney or Ford. These businesses are known for their enduring legacy, not just because they were successful, but because they built something that continues to inspire and innovate.

12.1 Building a Legacy Through Your Business

Building a legacy starts with the understanding that your business should aim for longevity and purpose beyond immediate success. Short-term success might bring you quick wins and immediate financial gains, but it's the long-term legacy that ensures your business remains relevant and impactful. Walt Disney didn't just create animated films; he built a world of imagination and wonder that continues to inspire generations. Similarly, Ford didn't just manufacture cars; it revolutionized the automobile industry and set the standard for innovation and mass production.

To create a legacy-minded business, focus on sustainable practices and ethical operations. This means considering the long-term effects of your business decisions on the environment and society. For instance, adopting eco-friendly practices and ensuring fair labor conditions can significantly enhance your business reputation and longevity. Investing in community and social responsibility initiatives is another powerful way to build your legacy. Whether it's supporting local charities, sponsoring community events, or implementing programs that give back, these actions not only benefit society but also strengthen your brand and customer loyalty.

Creating a company culture that values longevity and purpose is crucial. This involves embedding core values into every aspect of your business operations, from hiring practices to customer interactions. Encourage your team to embrace these values and lead by example. A company culture rooted in strong values and a clear mission will naturally attract like-minded individuals who are committed to building a lasting legacy.

Documenting and preserving your business legacy is equally important. Maintaining detailed records and archives of significant milestones, achievements, and challenges can provide invaluable insights for future generations. Consider creating a company history book or timeline that chronicles your business journey. This not only serves as a source of inspiration but also helps preserve the essence of your brand. Developing a brand narrative that reflects the company's legacy can also be a powerful tool. Share stories that highlight your company's values, milestones, and impact on the community. This narrative can be woven into your marketing materials, website, and social media to reinforce your legacy.

Succession planning is a critical aspect of ensuring your business legacy continues. Identifying and grooming potential successors early on can help maintain continuity and stability. Look for individuals who share your vision and values and have the skills and passion to lead the business forward. Establish clear succession plans and protocols to ensure a smooth transition when the time comes. This includes defining roles and responsibilities, setting performance expectations, and providing ongoing training and mentorship.

12.2 Reflection Section: Identifying Your Legacy Vision

Take a moment to reflect on what you want your business legacy to be. Consider the following questions:

- What impact do you want your business to have on your community and industry?
- What values do you want to be remembered for?
- How can your business practices align with these values to create a lasting legacy?

Write down your thoughts and use them to guide your business decisions and strategies moving forward.

Communicating the legacy vision to future leaders is vital. Ensure your successors understand and embrace the legacy you've built. Share your vision, values, and long-term goals with them regularly. This can be done through meetings, workshops, and written documentation.

Encourage them to contribute their ideas and perspectives to keep the legacy alive and evolving.

Building a legacy through your business is a journey of dedication and purpose. It's about making decisions that not only benefit your business today but also ensure its relevance and impact for years to come. By focusing on sustainable practices, community initiatives, and strong company culture, you can create a lasting legacy that stands the test of time. Documenting your journey, planning for succession, and communicating your vision to future leaders are essential steps in preserving and evolving your legacy.

12.3 Adopting a Continuous Improvement Mindset

Continuous improvement is about making small, incremental changes that collectively lead to significant enhancements over time. It's not about sweeping reforms but rather about regularly tweaking and refining processes to achieve better results. Think of it as the philosophy that underpins successful businesses like Toyota and GE. Toyota's approach, known as Kaizen, involves everyone from the CEO to the factory floor worker in identifying inefficiencies and proposing solutions. GE, on the other hand, has embraced Six Sigma, a data-driven methodology that seeks to eliminate defects and improve quality. Both companies have thrived by embedding continuous improvement into their culture.

To foster a culture of continuous improvement, you need to encourage employee suggestions and feedback. Create an environment where everyone feels valued and heard. Set up suggestion boxes, regular brainstorming sessions, or even an internal forum where team members can share their ideas. Training and development programs are also crucial. Equip your team with the skills they need to identify inefficiencies and propose solutions. Regular workshops, online courses, and seminars can keep everyone up-to-date with the latest best practices. Cross-functional improvement teams can bring diverse perspectives to the table. These teams can tackle specific problems, brainstorm solutions, and implement changes.

Identifying areas for improvement requires a systematic approach. Conduct regular process audits and reviews to pinpoint inefficiencies. This can be as simple as walking through your operations and noting down areas where things could be smoother or more efficient. Use customer feedback to identify pain points. If customers consistently complain about the same issue, that's a clear sign that something needs fixing. Analyze performance metrics and key performance indicators (KPIs) to spot trends and areas that need attention. For example, if your delivery times are slipping, dig into the data to find out why and address the root cause.

Implementing and sustaining improvement initiatives can be challenging, but it's essential for long-term success. Start by developing a structured improvement plan with clear objectives. This plan should outline what needs to be done, who is responsible, and the timeline for completion. Allocate the necessary resources and support for these initiatives. This might mean investing in new tools, hiring additional staff, or providing extra training. Celebrate and recognize successful improvements to keep the momentum going. Acknowledge the efforts of those involved and share the results with the entire team. This not only boosts morale but also encourages others to come forward with their ideas.

12.4 Checklist: Steps to Foster Continuous Improvement

1) **Encourage Employee Suggestions:**
    o Create suggestion boxes or forums.
    o Hold regular brainstorming sessions.
2) **Implement Training Programs:**
    o Offer workshops, online courses, and seminars.

o   Keep the team updated with the latest best practices.

3) **Set Up Cross-Functional Teams:**
   o   Form teams to tackle specific problems.
   o   Encourage diverse perspectives.

4) **Conduct Process Audits:**
   o   Regularly review operations to identify inefficiencies.
   o   Note down areas for improvement.

5) **Use Customer Feedback:**
   o   Identify consistent pain points mentioned by customers.
   o   Address issues based on feedback.

6) **Analyze Performance Metrics:**
   o   Monitor KPIs to spot trends.
   o   Investigate and resolve underlying issues.

7) **Develop Improvement Plans:**
   o   Outline objectives, responsibilities, and timelines.
   o   Allocate necessary resources.

8) **Celebrate Successes:**
   o   Recognize and share successful improvements.
   o   Boost team morale and encourage further suggestions.

Embedding continuous improvement into your company culture involves everyone from top management to entry-level employees. By fostering a culture where suggestions are welcomed, providing regular training, and using data to identify areas for improvement, you can create a dynamic environment that continually evolves and improves. This mindset not only drives efficiency and quality but also keeps your business competitive in an ever-changing market.

12.5 Future-Proofing Your Business

Preparing for future challenges is a key component of sustaining long-term success. Future-proofing your business means anticipating changes and being ready to adapt, ensuring that your company remains relevant and resilient. Companies like IBM and Microsoft exemplify this. IBM, for instance, transitioned from a hardware-focused business to a services and consulting giant. Microsoft, once synonymous with desktop software, successfully pivoted to cloud computing and AI. These shifts didn't happen overnight; they were the result of strategic foresight and continuous adaptation. Statistics show that businesses investing in future-proofing are more likely to survive and thrive. According to a study by Deloitte, companies that proactively address future risks are 30% more likely to achieve long-term success.

To stay ahead of industry changes and trends, you need to conduct regular environmental scanning and trend analysis. This involves keeping a close eye on market conditions, technological advancements, and consumer behavior. Participate in industry think tanks and innovation hubs to gain insights and collaborate with other forward-thinking professionals. These platforms provide valuable opportunities to exchange ideas and identify emerging trends. Building a flexible and adaptable business model is also crucial. This means creating systems and processes that can easily pivot in response to new developments. Flexibility allows your business to seize opportunities and mitigate risks as they arise.

Investing in innovation and research and development (R&D) is vital for remaining competitive. Allocate a portion of your budget specifically for R&D activities. This investment can lead to the development of new products, services, and processes that keep your business ahead of the curve. Encourage a culture of experimentation and risk-taking within your team. This means fostering an environment where employees feel safe to propose and test new ideas without fear of failure. Collaborate with universities and research institutions to tap into cutting-edge knowledge and technologies. Partnerships with academic institutions can provide access to state-of-the-art research and a pool of talented individuals eager to innovate.

Building resilience against future disruptions involves developing robust risk management and contingency plans. Identify potential threats to your business, such as economic downturns, supply chain disruptions, or technological failures, and create strategies to address them. Diversify your products, services, and revenue streams to reduce dependence on a single source of income. This diversification acts as a buffer against market fluctuations and helps maintain stability. Investing in technology and infrastructure upgrades is another way to build resilience. Ensure your systems are up-to-date and capable of supporting your business as it grows and evolves. Modern technology not only improves efficiency but also enhances your ability to respond quickly to changes.

12.6 Exercise: Future-Proofing Checklist

- Conduct regular environmental scanning and trend analysis.
- Participate in industry think tanks and innovation hubs.
- Build a flexible and adaptable business model.
- Allocate budget and resources for research and development.
- Encourage a culture of experimentation and risk-taking.
- Collaborate with universities and research institutions.
- Develop robust risk management and contingency plans.
- Diversify products, services, and revenue streams.
- Invest in technology and infrastructure upgrades.

Anticipating and responding to future trends requires a proactive approach. Regularly reviewing industry reports and market analyses helps you stay informed about potential shifts. Engage in continuous learning by attending conferences, workshops, and webinars that focus on future trends. Networking with other entrepreneurs and industry experts can provide valuable insights and help you identify emerging opportunities. Building a culture of continuous learning within your organization ensures that your team stays knowledgeable and adaptable.

Innovation doesn't happen in isolation. By fostering collaboration and encouraging diverse perspectives, you can create a fertile ground for new ideas. Involve employees from different departments in brainstorming sessions and innovation projects. This cross-functional approach brings together varying viewpoints and expertise, leading to more comprehensive and effective solutions. Recognize and reward innovative efforts to motivate your team to keep pushing boundaries.

Investing in technology is more than just upgrading your software. It's about integrating technology into every aspect of your business to drive efficiency, enhance customer experiences, and create new value propositions. Consider how technologies like artificial intelligence, machine learning, and the Internet of Things can be applied to your operations. For example, AI can help optimize supply chains, while IoT devices can provide real-time data on product performance. By leveraging these technologies, you position your business to adapt quickly and stay competitive.

Building resilience also means preparing for the unexpected. Develop contingency plans for various scenarios, such as a sudden market downturn or a critical supplier going out of business. These plans should outline specific actions to take and designate responsibilities to ensure a swift and effective response. Regularly review and update these plans to reflect changing conditions and new insights.

Diversification is another key strategy for future-proofing your business. By expanding your product or service offerings, you reduce reliance on a single revenue stream. This not only mitigates risk but also opens up new growth opportunities. Explore new markets, develop complementary products, or consider strategic partnerships that can enhance your value proposition.

Incorporating these strategies into your business practices will help you build a robust and resilient organization capable of navigating future challenges. By staying informed, fostering innovation, investing in technology, and preparing for the unexpected, you ensure that your business remains competitive and poised for long-term success.

12.7 Leveraging Mentorship and Networking for Ongoing Growth

When I first set out to create my own business, I quickly realized that going it alone was incredibly challenging. That's when I discovered the immense value of mentorship and networking. A strong mentorship relationship can provide you with invaluable guidance, fresh perspectives, and the wisdom that only experience can bring. Look at successful entrepreneurs like Mark Zuckerberg, who benefited from the mentorship of Steve Jobs. Jobs himself had the guidance of mentors like Mike Markkula, who played a pivotal role in Apple's early success. Statistics reinforce this: entrepreneurs with mentors are five times more likely to start a business and 20% more likely to experience growth. Networking is equally powerful. It's not just about who you know but also about how those connections can open doors to new opportunities, partnerships, and support systems.

Finding and building relationships with mentors might seem daunting, but it's more accessible than you think. Start by attending industry events and mentorship programs. These gatherings are fertile grounds for meeting experienced professionals who are often eager to share their knowledge. Platforms like LinkedIn can also be goldmines for connecting with potential mentors. Send thoughtful messages that highlight why you're reaching out and how their experience aligns with your goals. Don't be afraid to join mentorship platforms and networks, such as SCORE or MicroMentor, which specifically cater to connecting entrepreneurs with mentors.

Continuous networking is equally crucial. A vibrant network can provide ongoing support, new business opportunities, and valuable insights. Make it a habit to regularly attend industry conferences, meetups, and seminars. These events are excellent for building relationships with peers, customers, and suppliers. Engage actively in online communities and forums related to your industry. Platforms like Reddit, Quora, and specialized forums offer spaces where you can exchange ideas, seek advice, and stay updated on industry trends. Building these relationships takes time, but the payoff is substantial.

Maintaining and nurturing these relationships is where the real work lies. Schedule regular check-ins and updates with your mentors. This can be as simple as a quarterly coffee catch-up or a quick phone call to discuss your progress and challenges. Offering value in return is crucial to keeping these relationships reciprocal. Share your own insights, provide support where you can, and be genuinely interested in their endeavors. Participate in collaborative projects and initiatives that align with both your goals and those of your network. This not only strengthens your relationships but also opens up new avenues for growth and learning.

Networking isn't a one-time effort; it's an ongoing process that requires consistent effort and genuine engagement. By continuously expanding your network and maintaining strong relationships with mentors, you create a support system that can guide, challenge, and inspire you. This interconnected web of relationships becomes a powerful resource, providing you with the tools and insights needed to navigate the complexities of running a business.

In leveraging mentorship and networking, you build a foundation for sustained growth and resilience. The guidance and support from mentors can help you avoid common pitfalls and make informed decisions. Your network, on the other hand, offers diverse perspectives, opportunities for collaboration, and a sense of community. Together, they form a robust support system that enhances your ability to innovate, adapt, and thrive in an ever-changing business landscape.

Chapter 13
Conclusion

As we reach the end of this journey together, I hope you feel more prepared to take the leap into entrepreneurship. Let's take a moment to recap the key points we've covered throughout this book:

- Key Takeaways:
- Call-to-Action:
- Final Words of Encouragement

We began by laying the foundation, addressing the fear of failure, and setting clear business goals. Remember, overcoming fear is a natural part of the process, and setting SMART goals can guide your path. Identifying and validating your business idea is crucial, as is building a resilient mindset to weather the ups and downs.

We then moved on to crafting a solid business plan, a roadmap that will steer your business toward success. We delved into legal and administrative essentials, ensuring that you're well-prepared and compliant with necessary regulations. Funding your business can be a challenge, but we explored various options, from bootstrapping to finding investors and leveraging crowdfunding.

Setting up your operations is vital for efficiency and productivity. Selecting the right digital tools, creating a conducive workspace, and managing your time effectively can make a world of difference. Building a strong support network of mentors and peers can provide invaluable guidance and encouragement.

Marketing your business is all about developing a strong brand identity and crafting a digital marketing strategy. Utilizing social media and content marketing can help you reach and engage with your target audience. Sales strategies, including creating a sales funnel and mastering networking, are essential for attracting and retaining customers.

Managing finances is the backbone of your business. Effective budgeting, managing cash flow, understanding financial statements, and reducing costs are critical for financial stability. Scaling your business involves identifying opportunities, building a strong team, expanding your market reach, and leveraging technology.

Building a strong company culture and fostering employee engagement can drive your business forward. Navigating challenges, managing stress, and maintaining work-life balance are crucial for your well-being and long-term success. Finally, ensuring long-term success involves building a legacy, adopting a continuous improvement mindset, future-proofing your business, and leveraging mentorship and networking for ongoing growth.

13.1 Key Takeaways:

1) **Foundation & Planning:** Overcome fear, set clear goals, and validate your business idea. Your business plan is your roadmap.
2) **Legal & Financial:** Understand the legal requirements and manage your finances wisely.
3) **Operations & Marketing:** Use the right tools, create a strong brand, and engage with your audience through effective marketing.
4) **Sales & Growth:** Build a sales funnel, network effectively, and focus on scaling your business.
5) **Culture & Challenges:** Foster a strong company culture, manage stress, and maintain a work-life balance.

6) Long-term Success: Build a legacy, continuously improve, future-proof your business, and leverage mentorship and networking.

13.2 Call-to-Action:

Now it's your turn. Take the lessons and strategies we've discussed and apply them to your own entrepreneurial journey. Start by revisiting your goals and refining your business plan. Engage with your community, reach out to potential mentors, and begin building your network. Take small, consistent steps every day toward realizing your dream. Remember, success doesn't happen overnight, but with persistence and dedication, you can achieve your goals.

13.3 Final Words of Encouragement:

Starting and running your own business is one of the most rewarding things you can do. It's a journey filled with challenges, but also immense satisfaction. Remember my story: despite early failures and setbacks, I found the path to success and now enjoy a fulfilling life in Hawaii. You have the power to create the life you want. Believe in yourself, stay committed, and don't be afraid to ask for help when you need it. Surround yourself with supportive people, keep learning, and keep growing.

You've got this. Your journey to independence and freedom starts now. Take that first step, and don't look back.

References

- Percentage of Businesses That Fail
  https://www.lendingtree.com/business/small/failure-rate/
- Fear-Setting: The Most Valuable Exercise I Do Every Month
  https://tim.blog/2017/05/15/fear-setting/
- Setting SMART Goals for Your Small Business
  https://mailchimp.com/resources/smart-goals/
- Famous Entrepreneurs Who Succeeded After Failure
  https://www.business.com/articles/never-giving-up-9-
  entrepreneurs-and-millionaires-who-failed-at-least-once/
- 22 vision statement examples to help you write your own
  https://www.brex.com/journal/vision-statement-examples
- Market Research: How to Conduct It Like a Pro
  https://www.qualtrics.com/experience-
  management/research/market-research-guide/
- 8 Keys to Good Financial Plans
  https://www.schwab.com/financial-planning-collection/8-
  components-of-good-financial-plan
- Write your business plan https://www.sba.gov/business-
  guide/plan-your-business/write-your-business-plan
- Choose a business structure https://www.sba.gov/business-
  guide/launch-your-business/choose-business-structure
- common types of business licenses and permits | QuickBooks
  https://quickbooks.intuit.com/r/starting-a-business/permits-
  and-licenses/
- Business taxes | Internal Revenue Service
  https://www.irs.gov/businesses/small-businesses-self-
  employed/business-taxes
- Intellectual property: What it is, how to protect it
  https://smallbusinessresources.wf.com/intellectual-property-
  what-it-is-how-to-protect-it/

- From Zero to Millions: Case Studies of Bootstrapped Startups
  https://thesuccessfulfounder.com/from-zero-to-millions-case-studies-of-bootstrapped-startups/
- How to Find Angel Investors for Your Startup (7 Tactics)
  https://www.digitalocean.com/resources/articles/how-to-find-angel-investors
- Your Ultimate Guide to a Successful Kickstarter Campaign
  https://www.brandedagency.com/blog/tips-and-tricks-for-a-successful-kickstarter-campaign
- Microloans | U.S. Small Business Administration
  https://www.sba.gov/funding-programs/loans/microloans
- 20 Free & Paid Small Business Tools for Any Budget
  https://blog.hubspot.com/marketing/free-tools-run-business
- Office ergonomics: Your how-to guide
  https://www.mayoclinic.org/healthy-lifestyle/adult-health/in-depth/office-ergonomics/art-20046169
- 7 Time Management Tips for Entrepreneurs to Maximize ...
  https://wp.nyu.edu/mind/2024/03/20/7-time-management-tips-for-entrepreneurs-to-maximize-productivity-and-achieve-success/
- 8 Tips for Building Your Business Support Network
  https://www.sba.gov/blog/8-tips-building-your-business-support-network
- The Importance of Brand Identity
  https://www.topnotchdezigns.com/why-is-brand-identity-important-for-your-business/
- 9 Successful Digital Marketing Case Studies That Boosted
  .https://www.singlegrain.com/digital-marketing/9-successful-digital-marketing-case-studies/
- Social Media Marketing for Businesses
  https://www.wordstream.com/social-media-marketing
- 20 Content Marketing Examples That Stand Out in 2022
  https://blog.hubspot.com/marketing/marketing-examples-online-resources

- 11 Ultimate Sales Funnel Examples That Convert Like Crazy
  https://www.close.com/blog/sales-funnel-examples
- Why Networking in Sales Is So Important: 12 Tips
  https://www.acuitymd.com/blog/why-networking-in-sales-is-so-important-12-tips
- 13 Brilliant Customer Loyalty Program Examples
  https://clevertap.com/blog/customer-loyalty-program-examples/
- 27 Top Customer Feedback Tools for 2024
  https://blog.hubspot.com/service/customer-feedback-tool
- Why Your Small Business Needs A Budget
  https://www.forbes.com/councils/forbesbusinesscouncil/2022/02/07/why-your-small-business-needs-a-budget/
- 9 Best Business Budgeting Software Tools of 2024
  https://www.nerdwallet.com/best/small-business/business-budgeting-software
- 20 Strategies To Improve Cash Flow And Working Capital
  .https://www.forbes.com/councils/forbesfinancecouncil/2023/06/23/20-strategies-to-improve-cash-flow-and-working-capital-management-for-leaders/
- How to Read Financial Statements: A Beginner's Guide
  https://online.hbs.edu/blog/post/how-to-read-financial-statements
- Building Scalable Business Models
  https://sloanreview.mit.edu/article/building-scalable-business-models/
- The importance of core competencies and what they mean
  https://www.monkhouseandcompany.com/guides-resources/the-importance-of-core-competencies-and-what-they-mean-for-business-growth/
- How Startups Can Attract and Retain Top Talent
  https://www.hubspot.com/startups/attract-retain-top-talent
- The Vital Role of Technology in Business Scalability
  https://www.elorus.com/blog/business-scalability/

- ➢ Why are company values important? https://www.hays.net.nz/employer-insights/management-issues/why-company-values-matter
- ➢ Southwest Airlines: A Case Study in Employee Engagement https://www.entrepreneur.com/leadership/southwest-airlines-a-case-study-in-employee-engagement/280575
- ➢ Eight Ways to Build Collaborative Teams https://hbr.org/2007/11/eight-ways-to-build-collaborative-teams
- ➢ Fostering a Culture of Continuous Learning in the Workplace https://www.intellum.com/resources/blog/continuous-learning-in-the-workplace
- ➢ What Makes Entrepreneurs Burn Out https://hbr.org/2018/04/what-makes-entrepreneurs-burn-out
- ➢ How to Manage Stress with Mindfulness and Meditation https://www.mindful.org/how-to-manage-stress-with-mindfulness-and-meditation/
- ➢ How Netflix Faced A Digital Transformation: A Case Study https://sharpencx.com/netflix-digital-transformation-case-study/
- ➢ Famous Entrepreneurs Who Succeeded After Failure https://www.business.com/articles/never-giving-up-9-entrepreneurs-and-millionaires-who-failed-at-least-once/
- ➢ Building A Legacy: Key Steps To A Profitable And Enduring ... https://www.forbes.com/sites/melissahouston/2024/04/21/building-a-legacy-key-steps-to-a-profitable-and-enduring-business/
- ➢ What is Kaizen (Continuous Improvement)? https://www.techtarget.com/searcherp/definition/kaizen-or-continuous-improvement

➤ Better together: IBM and Microsoft make enterprise-wide
https://www.ibm.com/blog/better-together-ibm-and-
microsoft-make-enterprise-wide-transformation-a-reality/
➤ Data shows mentors are vital to small business success
https://www.nfib.com/content/benefits/management/data-
shows-mentors-are-vital-to-small-business-success/

Made in the USA
Las Vegas, NV
07 December 2024

12834070R00075